Getting Started With Holacracy

Getting Started With

HOLACRACY

Upgrading Your Team's Productivity

Diederick Janse / Marco Bogers

Copyright © 2020 by Diederick Janse & Marco Bogers

First paperback edition November 2020

Cover and interior design by Stewart A. Williams

ISBN 978 90 9033 523 0

FOREWORD

I've been a practitioner of Getting Things Done (GTD) for over ten years, and I love the clarity that practicing GTD has brought me. People often mistake GTD for just a cool way to organize lists, but I think the real secret sauce is that its distinctions and processes facilitate true clarity. The capacity to get clarity is the root of getting organized and certainly required for sustaining 'mind like water', as David Allen puts it. Once you can reliably and quickly generate clarity, productivity can't help but flow from that ground.

When you work in a team though, good clarity individually is just not enough. If anything, it heightens the pain. Because once you taste clarity, you become much more aware of when things are not clear. A next-action may be clear enough, but who on the team should take that action? Whose area of responsibility is it? When do you involve someone else, and when do you just take action yourself? All of those questions point back to a single challenge: how do we get clarity between us?

Working in a team demands another layer of clarity, beyond just individual clarity. When that clarity is lacking, all sorts of dysfunctional behaviors emerge that limit a team's productivity and flow. You may recognize some of them, because they happen in almost every team. One of them is seeking consensus or buy-in – when there's a lack of clarity on what authority you have to move ahead, perhaps you try to get your colleagues on board before you act. Another symptom of this lack of clarity is when people are constantly sending emails that CC everybody else. This is often a sign that you don't know who you actually need to talk to and why. Or maybe people are always looking to the boss to 'bless' a decision, because they're not sure what authority they have to use their own best judgment. Another symptom of lack of clarity is when you get frustrated with your colleagues for not meeting some implicit expectation that seems natural to you, but which they don't seem to share.

Earlier in my career, I was convinced there had to be a better way to work together. How do you get this 'mind like water' as a team, or even for the organization as a whole? That's a pretty big question, and it took me a long time to answer it. After many years of experimentation, a new approach emerged, through my efforts and those of many others. Holacracy, as it came to be known, is a new "social technology" for governing and operating a team or an organization. As Holacracy evolved, GTD became more and more influential in its systems and processes. As David Allen put it, "The parallels between GTD & Holacracy are legion – this is a way to get organizational mind like water. Holacracy takes everything that's unclear or that's not working as it could be, and channels it into clear and effective pathways to get clarity.

Some people mistake Holacracy for cool ways to run meetings, just like GTD often gets mistaken for cool ways to handle lists. But as any serious GTD practitioner knows, it's actually about changing the way you think about your work. It gives you a new language of projects and next-actions, words that have different and more clear meaning with GTD than they commonly do. Similarly, Holacracy gives you a language for clarifying team expectations and responsibilities. It changes the way authority works, and how expectations are set. These things are not just outputs of cool meeting processes; they change the fundamental structure of how power and authority flow, and ultimately how work gets done day to day.

And what happens when you put that new clarity to work in your organization? In over ten years of practicing GTD, I've seen that work doesn't decrease when I get better at processing my stuff into clarity and getting more done. Quite the opposite – when I have a really rockin' system and a 'mind like water', that creates space for all sorts of new problems and challenges. The same is true for organizations. When Holacracy helps you generate organizational 'mind like water', it just invites a new level of challenges to show up. Holacracy helps teams to get more done. And it helps them to do it in flow, instead of through the stress and politics that characterize many teams today.

And so I invite you to dive into this book to learn about Holacracy, from two of its earliest supporters in the Netherlands, Diederick Janse and Marco Bogers. I suspect you'll appreciate their perspectives if you hunger for more clarity and productivity in your team.

Enjoy the book!

Brian Robertson, pioneer of Holacracy
Birchrunville, Pennsylvania

CONTENTS

INTRODUCTION

T
eams waste countless hours in endless meetings, interruptions, and ad hoc work, not to mention that many people are drowning in their email. One of the questions we—a trainer and a consultant—have been asking ourselves is why it is so hard to actually be productive within the context of a team. Even if you succeed in being somewhat productive yourself, you are still always dependent on your team members. We often seem to work against each other, hence the blessing/curse: "I wish you lots of personnel." Yet, collaboration is the main source of productivity. In fact, the difference between being productive on your own and achieving a breakthrough in productivity as a team depends very much on how effectively you collaborate. This, ultimately, turns out to be the difference between success and failure at the team level.

Teams that are able to apply the art of collaboration can achieve unbelievable results. They bring out the best in people, create the conditions for optimum flow, and rise far beyond themselves. They have shown that even as a team it is possible to achieve the state of "a mind like water." There are many techniques and methods that promise to provide a solution for the challenge of cooperation and team productivity. Some of these include a course in time management for the entire team (based on David Allen's book *Getting Things Done*, for example, which we will discuss a little later), coaching the manager, or implementing Agile methods, such as Scrum. We tried a number of different approaches, but the lasting improvements we were looking for still eluded us. In our view, none of these approaches really dealt with the root of the problem. The challenges that teams wrestle with are not "defects" that can be fixed; they are the natural and inevitable result of the way in which teams and organizations are set up. The method described in this book is not a Band-Aid to be pasted onto this existing kind of structure; it is a wholesale replacement of it.

The key is in clarifying expectations and accountabilities, not just once, by a central authority (e.g. a manager), but continually and by the team itself. The method for this, which we will explain in this book, is called Holacracy. Holacracy is a method for team productivity that makes it possible to continually evolve the team structure based on small experiments and new information. Just as Getting Things Done (GTD) provides a complete upgrade for the way you set up your own workflow, Holacracy provides a comprehensive upgrade for the way teams and organizations work.

In this book, two threads are woven into one: a story thread and a theoretical thread. We chose this format because we wanted to write a book that can be read in just a few hours, without overly reducing the complexity of the subject matter. By reading the story, you will be able to relate to and easily absorb the method. You may also choose to go directly to the theory and read about the parts of the method that interest you. Or you can just read the story to get a first impression and then find more depth in the theory afterwards. It is up to you to decide how you want to navigate this book.

The central figure in the storyline is Neil, the manager of a marketing team. He has just landed a very promising deal that could mean a breakthrough for the company in the entire North American market. His team members are competent professionals, but the collaboration between them leaves something to be desired. As a consequence, he worries if his team will be able to pull off this new deal. Adopting Holacracy is like arriving in a new and fascinating country. If you want to understand local customs, you need to start by learning the language. Language is a crucial part of Holacracy. We will be introducing many new concepts in this book. They are summarized in a glossary at the back of the book, so you can easily consult them while reading.

This book would not have existed without the trailblazing work of the author and creator of *Getting Things Done*, David Allen, or of Brian Robertson, the creator of Holacracy. We are very grateful to them for their deep insights into the nature of work and cooperation. Many thanks also to Academic Service, the publisher of the original Dutch version of this book, without whose phone call we would have never come up with the idea to write this book. Many people directly and indirectly contributed to the creation of this book. We would like to express a special thank you to Job Creyghton. As our writing coach, he gave us the confidence to be able to write this book in this way and did a fantastic job guiding us in our writing process.

We hope you'll enjoy reading this book and especially that it will inspire you to start applying its ideas to your own team or organization.

Diederick Janse and Marco Bogers
Amsterdam, The Netherlands, July 2020

ONE

GETTING TEAMS DONE

THE DEAL

From the office in downtown Portland, Neil has an amazing view of the riverfront. On this spring-like day in February, the city seems on the verge of turning green. But the view is about the last thing on Neil's mind right now. Instead, he is thinking about the presentation he just finished. *Did I explain it properly? Should I have emphasized that one slide?* Rakesh, his boss, is sitting next to him.

Neil looks at him. "What do you think? Will we get the deal?"

"I'm not sure. They didn't say much. I'm not sure they share our vision for the Canadian market."

"I gave them all I've got."

"I know."

"It would be really great if my team could do this campaign. I feel we're close; we've got it, I'm sure."

"More importantly, if we get this deal, we'll turn a profit this year already," Rakesh grins.

The heavy door opens and the secretary asks them to come in. Neil feels his heart beating in his throat. They sit down at the big conference table.

Denis, the president, takes the floor. "We are impressed. We especially like the business case. We have therefore decided to introduce your Natural Cosmetics concept with a campaign in all of our North American stores."

"Thank you." A broad grin appears on Neil's face.

"Yes!" Rakesh pats Neil on the back. "Congratulations!"

"But, before we go on, we do want to make it clear that this will be a cross-media campaign." Denis fixes his gaze on the two men. "We will expect you to integrate all media in your execution."

"We have all the expertise we need for that," Neil says.

"And another thing. We want to start within four months. That means that the campaign has to be ready by July first. This is a crucial point for us. Are you able to guarantee this?"

For a moment there is silence.

"My understanding was that it was for August first," Rakesh says hesitantly.

"Change in priorities."

Rakesh looks at Neil, who is shuffling through his papers.

"We need an answer now." Denis says, smiling.

"Let me be honest; July first will be very tight. But we want to do this. In principle, I'd say the deadline is okay."

"In principle?" Denis looks at Neil.

"All right. Yes, we can do it."

"In our business, planning is everything. If we can't count on you, we have a problem."

"The first of July it is," Rakesh says.

"Okay, then we've got a deal."

○

On the 205 near the airport, the traffic is at its usual standstill. Neil looks at his watch. An hour and a half before their plane takes off.

After the meeting downtown, they immediately got into a taxi. Rakesh is talking on his cell phone nonstop. Neil still can't believe they got the deal. And for all of North America! If he does a good job on this, anything will be possible. He feels a bit dizzy just thinking about it. *Okay, Neil, take it easy. Put your feet back on the ground.* His mind wanders to his team; that deadline is going to be a problem.

Rakesh ends his phone call.

"Rakesh, that deadline is going to be pretty tight."

His boss turns to look at him. "Yes it's tight, but this is our big breakthrough. Just think about that. They could have gone with the competition …"

"No, no, of course we don't want that," Neil interrupts, "but …"

Rakesh's eyes follow a car as it zips into the lane right in front of them. "Lighten up already, we did it!"

Neil nods, but he has a slightly worried look on his face. "We've never done anything like this on such short notice. Our team's output is going to have to go up a notch!"

"Weren't you just telling me the other day about this system that helps people to be much more productive?"

"Yes, 'Getting Things Done.'"

"Can't you teach your team to use that?"

"I've tried already. It's really hard to break old habits."

"Well, that's what being a manager is: bringing out the best in your people!"

"Okay, well, we'll find a way to do it." Neil is trying to sound self-assured but not really succeeding.

"That doesn't sound very convincing … your team will have to increase their productivity."

Neil remains silent.

"The trick is to learn to delegate," Rakesh says matter-of-factly.

"It's won't be easy, but it *can* be done," Neil says with a smile.

The taxi is moving again. It looks like they'll make their plane home.

1.1 DEALING WITH TENSION

The deal is made. Now Neil will have to deliver! Can you imagine how he feels? From one minute to the next, you suddenly see a wave of opportunity and new horizons. At the same time though, you can also see how far you will have to go. There is a gap between where you are and where you need to get to. In Neil's case, the gap is pretty significant, so he is feeling a healthy dose of tension. This tension is what we will talk about next. It is at the heart of our story.

What is tension?

Tension is often seen as something negative. Just look at Neil. He has some pretty mixed feelings—of course he's happy to have landed the deal, but he fails to see just how his team will manage to deliver on it. The feeling of not being in control of a situation creates tension. It's not a great feeling, so most of us want to get rid of it as soon as possible. Everyone has their own way of dealing with tension. Some people want to fix the problem immediately, others prefer to step back and think about it, while others again try to ignore the whole thing entirely. No matter how different these strategies are, they are all based on the same assumption: that tension is a problem. But is that really true? What exactly *is* tension? The term "tension" usually refers to a sense of stress or excitement. It is the opposite of "relaxation," which refers to a sense of peacefulness.

We usually experience tension as a problem that we want to get rid of as soon as possible.

In this book, we will use the term in a different and more specific way: by "tension", we mean the difference between 1) how things are and 2) how they could be. The difference can be big or small. The bigger the difference, the greater the tension. If there is no gap between how things are and how they could be, then you are exactly where you want to be and you don't feel any tension. Electric tension is a pretty good metaphor—the greater the difference in electric tension between two poles, the greater the (electric) charge.

But what exactly are we talking about when we say "how things are" and "how they could be"? Maybe you're in a meeting and you're experiencing tension about how the meeting is going. You notice how it is now ("This meeting is not accomplishing anything") and how it could be ("We should be talking about what really matters"). But it can also be a small thing, for example, the front door sticks (how it is now), instead of opening and closing smoothly (how it could be).

Tension is the experience of a gap between how things are and how they could be

Tension is information

When you look at it this way, tension is a neutral thing. You notice that something is different from the way it could be. Such an experience only becomes positive or negative when you put a label on it. If you say, "This is how it *should* be," then it feels like negative tension to you; it feels like a problem. If you say,"This is how it *could* be," then it feels more like something positive, an opportunity, for example. This labeling is entirely subjective. Take Neil and Rakesh as an example. Neil is not sure his team will be able to meet the deadline, and therefore he experiences stress, a negative tension. Rakesh sees an opportunity to turn a profit this year, so he labels it as something positive. A discussion about who is "right" would be fruitless. After all, this is not about facts, but about different interpretations! A more interesting question is what you *do* with that tension because tension is really *information* about where you are now and where you could be.

> *Tension provides information about where you are now and where you could be*

Sometimes it is crystal clear what you need to do with that information; at other times, it is not so obvious. When there is high complexity, it can be difficult to interpret tension. Complexity is a fact of life for most of us. If you do mostly physical work, you can *see* when something is finished or what still needs to be done. But when it comes to knowledge work, those boundaries are less clear. Knowledge work demands thinking. Where am I right now? Where do I want to go and when am I done? What tension do I feel about where I am right now? Are there problems or opportunities, and how do I deal with them?

Whether or not you ask them consciously, most people wrestle with questions like these every day. Just because we do more and more knowledge work doesn't mean that we are automatically good at thinking. Knowledge work results in tensions that can be a little different from those resulting from physical work. They are often more complex, their boundaries are much less clear, and they exist in your head. You can't see them. The thinking involved in knowledge work is hard work and definitely does not take care of itself.

Knowledge work requires thinking, because it involves tensions that are a lot less visible

A good bricklayer has skills and habits. Although one person may have more of a talent for bricklaying than someone else, it still takes a lot of practice to get good at it. It is no different for knowledge work. The knowledge worker has skills and habits that he or she uses to carry out knowledge work. Personal effectiveness, setting goals, time management, communication, delegating, providing feedback, leadership—all these may come into play. An entire new industry has sprung up around these subjects in the past few decades.

Relaxed productivity

One of the most successful authors in the field of productivity and knowledge work is David Allen. His book *Getting Things Done* helped Neil (and millions like him) to get a grip on his work and to maintain it. Although Allen does not literally speak about tension, he does use a comparable term: *stuff*. To him, stuff is anything that is not (yet) where it should be. This may be the lawnmower, which is on the lawn instead of in the storage shed, or 10,000 unique visitors to a website when there could be 100,000. As you can see, "stuff" looks a lot like "tension." There are some subtle differences, but for the sake of convenience, we will be using the terms interchangeably here. When you don't know what to do with tension and stuff, you feel out of control. That feeling, or even the mere *idea* of losing control, directly leads to stress. The core of *Getting Things Done* is to treat tension in such a way that you can achieve a state of *relaxed* productivity, instead of one of stressful productivity.

> *Getting Things Done is a method that helps you to be*
> *productive in a relaxed way*

Just imagine that you could remain relaxed even in the face of the greatest, most complex tensions and that you could effectively deal with this *in flow,* or as Allen says, with "a mind like water"—completely in the moment, effortlessly effective. Quite the challenge for Neil, after his meeting in Portland!

THE SYSTEM

At the Portland International Airport, everything happens quickly. The screen says that their flight is leaving in forty-five minutes. Neil calculates that he can be home in just over two hours.

Rakesh has a seat in a different part of the airplane. The seat next to Neil is still empty. He rubs his eyes. It feels like they've got sand in them. He got up at five o'clock this morning.

A man sits down beside him and barely manages to squeeze his long legs in. Neil nods, and the man nods back with a slight smile as he pulls a shiny iPad out of his bag. A few minutes later, his fingers are flying across the screen. Out of the corner of his eye, Neil notices that the man is using the same software he uses. He turns to his neighbor.

"How do you like it?"

"Excuse me?"

"The software?"

"Oh … great. It's nice to work with."

"Let me introduce myself: Neil Holzer."

"John Perotti. Nice to meet you."

"Looks like you're a Getting Things Done user, is that right?"

"Yes, I've been using it for ages. Ever since the book came out, in 2001."

"I've been using it for the past year and a half. This book really changed my life." Neil's voice sounds almost solemn.

"I know what you mean! And is it working for you?"

"Well, I *am* getting more done, but, well …"

"Still not fast enough?"

"No, it's not so much that …" Neil hesitates; for a moment there is silence. Then he tells John about the new contract and how exciting it is, only to then apologize. "Sorry, I'm boring you."

"No, not at all," John smiles. "Go on!"

Neil tells him a bit about the doubts he has been having about the productivity of his team. "I had hoped that if I became more productive, the team would follow, but sometimes it seems like my attempts are having the opposite effect. And for this job, I'm definitely going to need greater productivity. So that's a problem for me."

"And you're wondering if Getting Things Done would be able to kick up your team's productivity a few notches?"

"I love it when I can do something faster with less effort." Neil explains how he wants to automate his "waiting for" list with delegated items, so that he will be able to delegate more and with greater ease. John turns to face him.

"Those are good tricks. But I think you are are still missing the essence of what you're looking for." Neil looks at John quizzically. "With all due respect, what you call delegating is really dumping." Neil looks a little offended, but John continues, unperturbed. "That only increases your problems. Especially if you say that your team is not as organized as you are."

"Do you have a system that works better?"

"You could call it a system, but it's not a trick I can just quickly show you on the spot. You're welcome to have a look at my action lists, but that won't tell you very much."

Neil gives John another puzzled look.

"It's not so much about lists; it's more about getting aligned. It's about the team having a conversation about how to work together.

It's really about communication and decision-making."

"But delegating is just organizing things efficiently and checking to make sure that what you've asked for is being done, isn't it?"

"If you're doing that, then you're viewing your job as manager more like breaking down the work and monitoring the output. And those are exactly the things that are better left to a team to do."

"I'm not so sure about that. My team already has a lot of freedom. I think maybe even too much. And that's why we don't actually end up collaborating that much."

They are above Seattle by now, and the plane makes a steep turn to begin the landing process. John packs up his things.

"It looks to me like you've got a huge challenge in front of you, Neil. To be honest, I'm not sure if the way you want to tackle it is going to work for you and your team."

"What would you do?"

"Give me a call sometime and we can talk about it." John gives Neil a business card and shakes his hand.

O

Neil walks into the Starbucks at 12th and Columbia with his laptop bag over his shoulder. He is greeted by the barista, who recognizes him from his usual Friday morning visit. He orders a venti latte, sits down in a big leather armchair near the window, and opens his laptop. He skips checking his email and goes directly to his task management program.

His "weekly review" is sacred—one hour by himself, during which he reflects on his work. He intentionally doesn't do it at the office because he gets easily distracted there.

A list of projects appears on the screen. He scrolls down: seventy items. He sighs deeply. He has put a lot of effort into his system lately. It feels like he's finally getting a handle on it. But is he going to be able to keep it all under control with this new campaign added to the mix? Will he be able to delegate better and faster? Or is that not the solution, as John suggested on the plane?

He looks at his "waiting for" list, with its outstanding and delegated actions. Most of the items have been on there for weeks, some even months. Damn, why doesn't everyone just do what they're supposed to? He has sent Tamara a reminder for the nth time and his request is still open. What's going to happen when the North American campaign is added? Should he have spoken up when Rakesh was so quick to agree to the deadline? He's beginning to feel more and more discouraged. After taking another sip of coffee, he focuses on the screen again and opens the spreadsheet that contains the capacity planning. Maybe he can use that to calculate how much capacity they will need in the next few months. His fingers almost automatically begin to move on the keyboard. Once he's working with Excel, he can get completely absorbed, especially when he is really trying to get things to line up.

This time, he just can't get it to work.

Frustrated, he closes his laptop and just stares straight ahead for a while. Eventually, he notices a local artist's work on the walls—naturalistic pen and ink drawings of Seattle views. Good idea. Putting things on paper always helps him to think more clearly. He finds a notebook in his bag and starts to write. After a few minutes, the page is full of underlined and circled words, lines, and scratches. ...

His mind is emptying. Gradually things begin to look a bit clearer.Neil sighs and smiles. He does not have to take all this on his own shoulders; he does not have to solve everything himself. He can just share it with the team and ask them for their input.

1.2 GETTING THINGS DONE

The world never stands still. No matter how organized you are, reality will always catch up with you. While you are reading this, your inbox is filling up with new emails. Your calendar is full of meetings and appointments with other people. Maybe you keep a list of all the things you still have to do, or you have some other way of keeping track of your work. Everyone does it in their own way, and for some it is easier than for others. Neil's problem is one that most of us recognize. You have a bunch of things under control and you know exactly what you are doing. But then something unexpected happens and suddenly you are once again struggling just to get on top of it all. Your thoughts start to go in all different directions and are constantly distracting you. I have to think of this, remember that ... And this has to be finished, and I have to organize that ... Stress!

The sense of losing control leads to stress

The problem with stress is that it makes you reactive. You can no longer see the forest for the trees, so it's hard to separate the important things from the minor issues. You are no longer choosing where to put your attention; it is taken up by the most urgent problem, your unread email, or the person with the loudest voice. One alternative is to create a detailed plan for everything you have to do and when to do it. Everything has its place, and then it's just a matter of sticking to your plan. Unfortunately, this is not as simple as it sounds: reality rarely sticks to your plan! So how *can* you deal with the complexity and dynamics of your work? Do you have to accept stress as a necessary side effect of productivity? Or is it possible to be productive from a place of relaxation, with your attention fully focused and a calm, clear mind?

Empty your mind

As long as your mind is brimming with thoughts and open loops, you will not be able to relax. Whether you call it stuff or tension, it is distracting and it creates stress. The essence of Getting Things Done is to empty your mind so that you can consciously decide what is important now (see Appendix 1 for a summary of the method). But why does everything have to be outside of your mind? Why do you need an empty mind? Doesn't chaos lead to creativity? You have a limited working memory, so your mind is not the best place for keeping *everything* that is important. It will continuously remind you of open loops, whether there is anything you can do about them right now or not. During the meeting, you suddenly remember that you have to buy ink for the printer. And when you're sitting on the couch at home, your thoughts keep returning to next week's presentation. Hardly the best use of a resource that you have only a limited amount available of each day: your attention!

The essence of Getting Things Done is to empty your mind so that you can be productive from a place of relaxation

Relaxed productivity - how do you do it?

Emptying your mind is the first step, but it doesn't stop there. What do you do with each of those open loops? GTD suggests that you give them a place on a number of lists, which together will form a systematic overview of what's on your plate. Then you don't have to look at them again until the right time and place. In order to keep that system current and reliable, you regularly update it. Finally, based on this complete and updated overview, you decide what you want to do now (and, just as important, what you are *not* going to do now). A big part of GTD deals with how you set up a system like this in a really smart way. The short version of that is you maintain a number of different lists. Neil's "waiting for" list is a good example. He puts everything that he is waiting for from others on this list. These items could be tasks that he has delegated within his team, but it could also be the reply he's awaiting to the important email he sent last week. How you organize these kinds of lists has become a source of much popular debate on the internet.

If you do a search for "GTD," you will find tons of software and tips. But if you think this is all about smart tools, you're missing the point. GTD is a set of habits and skills that you acquire by practicing them. Of course, it helps if you use good tools, but the essence of relaxed productivity lies not in the tools, but in the thinking habits that GTD "installs."

GTD is more than smart lists and funky tools; it is a set of thinking habits

THE TEAM

I t's nine o'clock on Monday morning. One by one, the team members trickle into the meeting room on the twenty-fourth floor of Qwest Plaza. There is just enough room for all seven members of the marketing team. Neil hands out today's agenda and the minutes from the last meeting.

"Is Suzanne coming?"

"I just saw her," Will says.

"Okay, we'll wait for her."

Meetings rarely start on time; something Neil has come to accept. Five minutes later, Suzanne walks in with a cup of coffee in her hand.

"Sorry, guys, I really need my shot of caffeine to get started."

Suzanne is a woman in her thirties. She always wears pumps, so you can hear her approach from a distance. "Hey Neil, how was Portland last week? Did you have a nice hotel?"

"Better than that: we got the deal!"

"Wow!" Suzanne says, and gives him a thumbs up. "And they agreed with the budget?"

"Yup."

"Yes! I'm telling you, if I get to make a commercial on this budget, I'm going for nothing less than a Clio award."

"Hold on a minute," Neil interrupts her, a little abruptly. "I'd like to explain what we agreed on first." In a few sentences, he tells them what was discussed in Portland and particularly emphasizes the fact that the deadline has been moved forward. "And that means that we have to be done in four months." He gives Suzanne a pointed look and pauses before he continues. "Rakesh feels that it should be doable; I myself am not so sure if we will be able to do it. But he wants an answer from me today." Again, he pauses for a moment. "And ... on top of all that the campaign will be for all of North America, including Quebec and Mexico City. Everything has to be created in three languages and it will be run in three different countries."

"I don't see any problem with that," Suzanne says. "I'll have that ad agency lined up in no time, we can shoot a commercial in a month, and ..."

Neil interrupts her again. "This is different, Suzanne; this is really big."

"So? We can do it!"

Will, who is accountable for the stores, enters into the discussion. "This is not just about shooting a commercial. I think it's important for us to design some really good displays. The focus should be on the stores, because that's where the purchasing decisions are made."

"And what about online and mobile?" Tamara, the internet marketer, pipes up. A few moments later, everyone is talking at the same time.

Neil raises his voice to be heard above the din. "Everyone, stop, please! We won't get anything done this way. We still need to discuss the details of the campaign. That's not something we'll get done this morning. What we need to do right now is figure out whether we can take this on in addition to what we already have lined up for the next quarter."

Everyone is quiet for a moment.

"I have added the overview of our capacity planning to the

minutes; I assume it's up to date?"

Tamara picks up the print-outs from her stack. "Sorry, Neil, but those sheets of yours are just too much hassle. If I have to keep track of all of that …"

"What do you mean?"

"I tried it the first few weeks, but I really don't know how to keep up with all of this. Plus, I have no idea what my days are going to be like, let alone the coming weeks. Our work just can't be planned."

"Yeah, same here," Suzanne calls out.

Neil feels his anger rising. He has put a lot of time into this system. "And you're telling me this now? We all said we were going to do it! I don't hear Soraya and Lien complaining, do I?"

"Because, with all due respect, their work is a lot more routine than mine or Tamara's," Suzanne answers matter of factly.

Tamara continues, "If I had to fill out that system of yours all the time, it would take me several hours a week. Sorry, but I don't have time for that."

"Why haven't you told me about this before? Why do I have to keep asking about it?"

"I told you before that I didn't like it, but you didn't want to listen."

Neil's face is turning red and he takes a deep breath. He knows Tamara; if he responds to this, it will be an endless discussion.

"Okay, let's get back to the campaign for a moment. Can we do it in four months?"

Silence.

Finally, Suzanne says, "It's a cool project. But I don't know if it can be done in that timeframe. You decide; after all, you're all about the planning."

O

Neil walks back to his desk. There is a big whiteboard on the wall, full of Post-its, magnets, and bits of paper. Most of it is no longer current: with one motion, he pulls all the print-outs off the board and throws them in the waste basket. He sits down at his desk in the corner of the open office. His desk is empty: just a computer with an inbox. He is tempted to dive into his email. Don't do it! Okay, so do what, then? He is feeling irritated, pressured. Can he still back out? No, of course not! Soraya, his research assistant, has settled at the desk across from him.

"You tell me, Soraya. Why can nobody plan their work around here?" His irritation is audible.

"Hmm."

"Well, what do you think?"

"I've known the team for a while. They're a creative bunch. They do their best work when they have a lot of space. Planning kills creativity."

"That may be so, but I really want to ace this campaign! I need to be sure that we can pull it off." Neil stares in front of him.

From the moment he was given charge of this department, he has been trying to bring structure into the work, without much success. Now he wonders: should he go along with the chaos, or enforce more discipline? Maybe he should include it in everyone's performance evaluation?

"You seem to take planning very seriously." Soraya looks at him. "Don't get me wrong; I understand planning is important, but you really make it into a major issue." "That's my job."

"But it's fantastic we got the deal, right? We'll make it; don't worry. The team is very flexible."

"Yes, a bit too flexible," Neil sighs. "And I'm still stuck with Rakesh expecting an answer from me today." He gets up, walks to the window and back again. "Soraya, I'm thinking: maybe I'm over-complicating things. I'll just ask everyone to email me an overview of their projects this afternoon. They don't have to stick with my planning, but at least that will give me some insight."

"Good idea!"

Neil opens his email program and begins to type.

FRUSTRATION

At the end of the day, Neil is tired. He's been in a meeting all afternoon. He sits down at his desk; one more hour before everyone goes home. Just enough time to check his email and see if he can make sense of the campaign planning for the next few months. He looks at the emails that have come in that afternoon, until he ends up with just the replies from his team to his request for a project overview. He notices he's one short: Suzanne's.

He takes a quick walk around the office, but he can't find her. He asks around if anyone has seen her. "She was in a meeting with the ad agency all afternoon!" Lien calls out. Lien is a copywriter and Suzanne's assistant. She takes care of the blogs and social media within the team. Neil starts to feel more and more annoyed. He sends Suzanne a text asking her to come and see him after the meeting.

Suzanne is sloppy with her email. He knows this, but he can't get used to it. He hears the clicking of high heels; a moment later Suzanne walks into the office.

"Suzanne, I sent you an email asking for a project overview."

"What email is that?"

"The one from this morning. I sent it right after our meeting."

She sits down at her computer and scrolls down. "Oh, right. I see it. But you don't have to send me an email for that, do you? You already know what I'm working on, right?"

"No, I don't, actually. Not exactly."

"Well, I can just tell you." Suzanne mentions the campaigns she is working on. Neil sighs, but she continues as if she didn't hear him. "Oh, and, right, I forgot to tell you about that. Did you know we have a deal with one of the local network affiliates?" she looks at him with big eyes. "They want to interview me for the lifestyle program. I didn't tell you? Sorry, this must have been when you were in Portland."

"That's great. An interview is always good publicity. And when is this happening?"

"Next Friday will be the first one."

"What do you mean, the first one?" There is an undertone of worry in Neil's voice.

Suzanne tells him that it is a weekly broadcast and she will be giving a short interview about the products each time. Neil starts to feel more and more uncomfortable.

"You mean you're going to be out of the office for part of the day every week?"

"Yup, and there's some really well-known local people working on it," Suzanne replies, beaming.

"But that's going to take up a lot of your time and you're already far too busy!" Neil notices Will sitting at his desk and calls him over."I'd like to know exactly what this deal entails."

Will explains that it involves a large amount of sponsor funds and that for each broadcast a discount is offered on a product. "It's a wonderful opportunity; the editor absolutely wants us in the program."

Neil interrupts him. "But we have talked about this! Our target group doesn't watch these kinds of programs. They show cheap cosmetics during the same show and we want to focus on the luxury segment!"

"They have a huge reach; two million people watch that show." Suzanne flicks an imaginary piece of dust from the desk.

"And we have to reach our sales this quarter. My sales targets are a stretch," Will says.

"With all due respect, you agreed with those targets yourself at the time. And that was without any discount. You're supposed to be selling products; not giving them away with a discount. And besides, those discounts get taken out of the marketing budget. And you should have checked that with me first. I am responsible for the expenses."

"Two million viewers a week. We'd be insane to say no to that, wouldn't we?" Will sounds indignant.

Now Neil is really starting to feel angry. "If it's not our target group, it's throwing money away. And then you give them a discount on top of it! There goes our carefully developed brand image."

Suzanne and Will are quiet now.

"Well, just forget it. I'm going home." Neil gets up, grabs his coat, and walks out of the office.

O

It's freezing cold out. Usually he can leave his work behind, once he gets on his bicycle, but he can't seem to let go of the conversation with Will and Suzanne. What makes them think they can just go ahead and agree to a deal like that? Without even consulting him! Should he ask them to back out? But that would cause a lot of bad feelings. On the other hand, they need everyone and all resources to get this North American campaign on track. And this is certainly not helping. He slowly shakes his head. Is he being too rigid? It's good that they're pulling in publicity, after all. Shouldn't he be giving them more freedom? Judge them by the results at the end of the road? No, the team is already so scattered and that would only make it worse. It wouldn't have to be this way if they sent in their information on time. When he hears about something in retrospect, there is not much he can do to adjust things. That is why he tries to get everyone to fill out the planning, but so far, he has not had very good results.

He thinks back to the talk he had with John Perotti during his plane trip from Portland. A productivity system for teams. It sounds good to him right now. Didn't he take John's number? He stops, gets off his bike, and searches in his phone. There it is! He makes the call.

1.3 LIMITS OF GTD

Neil and his team are facing a huge task. They have what it takes, but it has to be done in four months. Their productivity will have to increase a lot for them to be able to meet this deadline. Getting such a complicated campaign off the ground will only work if the entire team gets behind it. But that is easier said than done! Listening to some of the team's discussions, it sounds like they still have a long way to go. What should the campaign look like? Is it feasible to do it within four months? What is the most important part and where do they start? And what exactly is expected from whom? Whether you talk about it or not, everyone has their own take on these questions. Aligning mutual expectations is one of the hardest things about collaboration. You know how those discussions go: "I thought you were going to take care of that ..." "Didn't you say that you ...?" And making the actual decision is harder still. What decisions do we make together? And how do we make them? If you want to be part of a great team, you must answer these questions.

Aligning expectations is one of the hardest things about collaboration

Working in teams

Neil's first reflex is understandable: he wants to provide more direction—better planning, better delegation, and then staying on top of everything to make sure everything gets done. The team is less happy about his approach though. "Don't distract us with all of your planning, and stop trying to micromanage us. We know how to do our job!" It is not easy to make a team perform. An army of coaches, trainers, and consultants make their daily living off of it—let's send everyone on a time management course! Or maybe we should do some process improvement! Job descriptions; that's what we need around here! Or, maybe we just need to get away from it all! An offsite day, a bit of team-building; that's how we will achieve our goals! The approach is always the same: once we clarify what is expected of everyone, everything will just fall into place. Whether it is processes, job descriptions, or the vision, with clear expectations and agreements, everything will make sense, or at least we can keep going for some time.

In a stable and predictable environment, such approaches can work, at least for a while. But if your environment is complex and constantly in flux, these approaches break down rapidly. The best-case scenario is that they will provide some temporary relief. Often it looks good on paper, but it only provides an illusion of control. Chaos is an option too, of course. You often see this with start-ups: "Let's not waste our time on endless meetings and organizational structure. That will just stifle our creativity and slow us down." What ends up happening pretty soon is that informal structure emerges, in which the people with the loudest voice get their way. It takes a lot of energy to keep that going. And even if you succeed, chaos and informal structure do not scale well.

Team productivity

Meanwhile, Neil is stuck with the deadline. Is the team going to manage the necessary leap in productivity? Everyone works very hard, but individual productivity does not necessarily make a productive team! This really shows in the team's discussions; they all talk over each other, jump from one topic to another, and when time is up, no real decision has been made.

Such lack of clarity causes confusion and frustration. The conflicts resulting from the diversity in the team begin to feel more and more personal. Some team members will push their agenda, while others withdraw. Meanwhile, the team makes no progress.

A group of productive people does not necessarily make a productive team

Why is it so difficult? Managing your own individual work-load can be complicated enough, but whether you do it with or without GTD, most people do succeed in being reasonably productive! Team productivity, however, requires an extra ingredient: alignment. Or, as the Sufi's say: *Because you understand "one," you believe you also understand "two," because one plus one equals two. But you also have to understand "plus."* Alignment and clarity on expectations are the essence of team productivity. Hiring the occasional consultant to optimize processes or lead an offsite is not enough. Nor is letting things slide and hoping they'll eventually work themselves out.

Just as Neil organizes his own work with GTD, the team also needs a trusted system for alignment and collaboration in the team, a system that creates clarity and structure, that is flexible enough that it can be adjusted according to changing circumstances, but that also offers a clear picture of what the team wants to accomplish, what is expected from each person, and who is accountable for what—a system that ensures that decisions are made quickly, that different perspectives are integrated, and above all, that brings the entire team into a flow, so it can make a leap in productivity. What Neil needs is *Getting Things Done* for teams!

Team productivity is more than the sum of each individual's productivity; it requires a different approach

TWO

HOLACRACY

THE COACH

A s soon as Neil passes into the stately lobby of Columbia Center, the city's hustle and bustle disappear. He is greeted with a friendly smile by one of the formally dressed porters. When he phoned John earlier, it turned out he was in town and suggested meeting at his office. Neil takes the elevator to the sixty-seventh floor, where he finds John's company. They meet in the lounge, and Neil brings him up to speed about the recent state of affairs. He gets angry all over again as he tells him about the deal Will and Suzanne made. "It seems like everyone is just doing their own thing. I really don't know how to organize the campaign with this team."

"Hmmm," John nods.

"When we were in the plane, you said you have a system, a kind of Getting Things Done for teams."

"You could call it that."

"That's what I need!" Neil exclaims with so much fervor it makes John laugh. "I would love to have as much clarity in my team as I have for my own work."

"Yes, that's certainly possible."

"What I want is to have an overview of what everyone is doing and what the status of each person's project is, so that I know whether we're going to reach our goal as a team. Preferably with just one click."

"I'm not sure that's going to solve your problem," John says.

"Wait, take a look at this." Neil opens his laptop and shows John how his capacity planning sheet.

After a few minutes, John interrupts him.

"Yes, that looks great, but the system I'm talking about is not a system of lists and tables. There is a place for those, but that's not what this is. And those spreadsheets look nice, but they're not going to make the difference here."

Neil feels uncomfortable. "I created those spreadsheets with the help of a consultant. It was a lot of work. And it's working for other companies."

"That may be, but has it done anything for you so far?"

"Well, at least we don't have nearly as much chaos as we did a few months ago. I wouldn't want to go back to that."

"I can understand that."

"But I do need something. I need something I can use to create a reliable plan so that I can be sure that we can complete this campaign."

"It looks to me like you need more than a reliable plan."

"What do you mean?"

"A couple of things. From what you were saying before, it sounds like you have unclear expectations in your team, decision-making is painful, and you lack focus. Am I right?"

"Yes," Neil admits as he's studying his hands.

"Look, what I think you're missing, if you want to call it a system, is an 'operating system' for the team. That is something else entirely than what you have now."

"You mean something like Windows or Mac OS?'

"Something like that, but adapted to a team. Call it a social technology. It includes rules about how the team collaborates, how to set priorities, and how to make decisions."

"And does it have a name?"

"Holacracy."

"Hola ... what?"

"Holacracy. I know; it's an unusual word. I had to get used to it too. It was developed by an American entrepreneur who was familiar with both Getting Things Done and Agile."

"So how does it work?"

"Everything in Holacracy starts with 'tension.' Things are not going the way you want them to. Kind of what you are experiencing with your team right now."

"You mean everybody doing their own thing."

"Yes, something like that," John says. "Closing a new deal is great, but it also creates lots of tension. With Holacracy, you can use this tension as fuel for moving forward and making this better. It helps you create extreme clarity within your team. And that's what you need in the situation you're in right now, between you, Will, and Suzanne."

"Use tension as fuel? What do you mean by that?"

"Look, tension is really just energy. Just like the gas you put in your car. But in teams, tension is usually wasted. That's what most people call conflict or friction. It's what slows down your team, or causes it to break down entirely."

"It sounds interesting, but I still can't really picture what you're talking about. How is it going to help me in organizing a campaign?"

"First of all, the alignment of the team will improve, because you will all know exactly who is accountable for what."

"That would be damn convenient, because it is not that unusual for people to duplicate work or, worse, for things not to get done at all," Neil comments eagerly.

"And that clarity enables teams to make quicker and better decisions and therefore to work faster. When you have a big project like your campaign, that's crucial. You can't afford to slow things down with painful decision-making."

"But what does it look like? Can I see it?"

"It is most visible in the meetings with your team. Every meeting will be crisp and effective. There's also some software that you can use. Just like the lists in Getting Things Done. For example, during one of the meetings you use a team board that you track everyone's progress on."

"We already have a board like that," Neil grins.

John continues, unperturbed, "What I mean is an visual management tool. You look at it and you instantly know how you're doing as a team."

"Sounds wonderful; I think I'm starting to get the picture." Neil's eyes begin to glow as he imagines how it would work. "But I still think it sounds complicated. What's the most important thing to know about it?"

"In essence, Holacracy is a way of running a team, or even an entire organization, in an agile and dynamic way, so that you can speed up on all fronts."

"So if I understand you correctly, I shouldn't be focusing on improving my capacity planning?"

John's face now has a mock helpless expression.

"All that effort ..."

"Hmmm."

○

It is late afternoon by the time Neil is walking back to his office. Crossing Pike Street, he nearly gets run over by a cyclist. His expectations of the meeting with John had been different. Couldn't John just have told him what to do?

Back at the office, Soraya is still working.

"How was your meeting?"

"Interesting. It certainly gave me food for thought. Do you think we make quick and good decisions?"

"Well, no, not really. I think it's mostly endless talk."

"I couldn't agree with you more. And I think we can't continue this way for the next few months."

"Do you have anything in mind?"

"This afternoon I spoke with someone that has a way of speeding it up."

"What do you mean by 'speeding up'?"

"Well, for example, that a meeting is quick and efficient and gives everyone energy instead of it keeping you from your work."

"That's music to my ears."

"I'm still not sure exactly how it works, but I am attracted to the idea." Neil opens his email in the meantime. "Now may not be the best time to make a change like that." His whole screen is filled with unread emails. "Still, I'd like to do something with it. But I'm concerned about how the team will respond; they are already up to their eyeballs in work."

He starts to process his email but stops right away and looks at Soraya. "This isn't working, is it? We're never going to make it." He looks at his screen again, and then pounds his desk with his fist. "You know what? I'm going to give it a try. What do we have to lose?"

"Do you think you can get everyone onboard?"

"I have no idea."

2.1 GTD FOR TEAMS

The benefits of Getting Things Done, but for the team as a whole? That's exactly what Neil needs! He is already doing GTD, so he just needs to adjust a few things, maybe pick up a few tricks, and then he will have the clarity he is looking for with his team! John quickly dispels his illusion though: team productivity is very different from individual productivity. Doing exactly the right things from a place of relaxation—that was the promise of GTD. As if that weren't enough of a challenge, collaborating with others adds a whole new dimension! Let's take Neil's team as an example: Everyone is doing their own thing, and when they get together, they fall over each other in their haste to express their opinion. There is lots of friction, conflict, and ego's clashing. Decisions are made with great difficulty or not at all. There are all kinds of implicit expectations flying around, and people feel stressed or disengaged. And what does Neil do? He's desperately trying to keep everything on track with more planning and more control.

Looking at it from that perspective, it is a miracle that they're getting anything done at all! Of course, there is a lot you can do to work in smarter, less painful ways. But if your team wants to get into flow and do exactly the right things from a place of relaxation, that's a quantum leap. Playing the game better is not going to do it. You have to start playing a different game entirely. Not finetuning your software with some good tips and tricks, but upgrading the operating system itself.

A truly productive team requires an operating system upgrade

Holacracy: a new operating system

Holacracy is that new operating system. It is a systematic approach for achieving team productivity, just as GTD is one for individual productivity. That comparison is not coincidental; the underlying principles of these methods are very similar. In particular, Holacracy derives from GTD the discipline and clarity of thinking, and the habits and skills that come with it. While in GTD you can do all of that by yourself, in Holacracy it becomes most visible in the team's meetings. After all, that's where the team aligns and makes decisions. In Holacracy, the team uses the meetings to create clarity about their work and how they do it. Each team member has lots of autonomy in how they get their work done, but that autonomy sits within a clear and explicit framework of roles and accountabilities. Those roles and accountabilities, in turn, are continuously adjusted and further clarified based on reality. And that's where another key source of inspiration comes in: Agile.

Continuous improvement

Agile is a collection of principles and ideas from the software world, which intends to create better software by leaning heavily on autonomy and flexibility. One of the best-known methods that falls under the Agile umbrella is Scrum, which is enjoying increasing popularity around the world. Agile's big breakthrough is that in a complex environment you should not do all the design upfront. If you do, you will not have the opportunity to make adjustments if something changes or if new insights emerge. Instead, you start with a small first step, then you adjust, and you make another small step. Holacracy applies this principle to teams instead of software, and particularly to its roles and accountabilities. Instead of designing these upfront, as is common in almost every organization (think org charts and job descriptions), you start with something workable, and then then adjust along the way, based on what reality tells you works or doesn't work.

Holacracy combines the discipline and clarity of GTD with Agile's flexibility

Holacracy calls this disciplined process of continuous improvement "dynamic steering."

Self-organization

Just like Agile, Holacracy involves the whole team in this process of continuous improvement. In a complex environment, you need everyone's knowledge and input. However, it is far from easy to integrate all those different perspectives and still keep the momentum going. Self-organization does not equal chaos; there is a definite need for direction and leadership. In Holacracy, however direction and leadership are not the domain of one centralized authority (i.e. a manager); rather, they are distributed. Each team member has one or more well-defined roles, in which they are not only accountable for certain areas of work, but also have full decision-making authority. Another way of looking at it, is that everyone both leads and follows, depending on the subject, instead of one person always leading and everyone else always following.

In Holacracy, direction and leadership are distributed, so that everyone is a leader within his or her own roles

You can look at these roles as the Agile version of a position or job description: they are not designed by management or HR, but instead created and continuously adjusted by the team itself. In this way, an organic structure emerges in which it is extremely clear what is expected of each team member, so everyone is free to spend their time and energy on getting the work done. It's like GTD's relaxation and flow, but for the team as a whole!

TENSION

Neil had never noticed the old factory in SoDo before. When John had agreed to the request for a presentation, he had suggested using his company's creative space in the Industrial District as a less formal location than Columbia Center. Neil walks into the brick structure and finds John on the second floor, putting the finishing touches on his presentation. The team members trickle in one by one. When they are all seated, Neil begins. He summarizes how he met John and that he was inspired by his method to make the team faster and better.

John gets up and stands in front of the group. "Good morning, everyone. I understand we have no time to lose, so let me just jump in right away. How many of you ever experience tension while you're at work?"

"Who doesn't?" Lien responds with a grin. The others laugh.

"You might as well ask when I don't." says Will.

John looks around the group. "Does anyone here have something specific on their mind?"

"Well, sure, now that you mention it." Will sounds slightly irritated. "I could sell a lot more if we introduced a few additional products for the mid and lower segments. I've been saying that for months."

Neil can't help but take this personally. He wants to react, but controls himself. No, this is not the right time. "What Will is saying, is *that* what you mean by tension, John?"

"Yes, exactly! It's an excellent example. And, by the way, Will, this is something I hear often. It's the eternal discussion between marketing and sales."

The example has helped John to get everyone's attention. He goes on to describe tension as energy that can be used to change something or set something in motion. "Tension is not necessarily a bad thing. A North American campaign is great, of course, but you have a lot of work already, so how are you going to pull it off? You're right in wondering about that. An ambitious goal, by definition, creates a stretch, or tension. Every question that you can't answer immediately creates tension. In fact, you could say that everything that you feel could be different from what it is now is a tension, in my definition."

Neil says, "John, when you put it like that I suddenly see that we deal with lots of tension all the time. But what does that have to do with team productivity?"

"Everything," John replies. "When tension is swept under the rug, it becomes like sand in the machine. And then everything gets tougher. But you can also use tension in a more productive way."

Will sits upright in his chair. "Well, I'd sure like to know how to do that."

"First of all, you have to notice it. Each of you actually acts as a sensor for tension."

"You mean like a radar?"

"Yes, something like that. You all have a built-in antenna that automatically picks up tension. And believe me, it's scanning all the time, even though most of you are probably not aware of it. So if you want to use that tension, the first step is to become aware of what you're picking up. To notice what it is that has your attention."

"You mean a kind of mindfulness?" Soraya asks.

"That's one way of putting it," John says.

"The second step is to do something with that tension, which I call 'processing' the tension. Processing a tension can be done in different ways, but one important way is to bring it to a team meeting."

John goes on to explain that there are two different types of meetings in Holacracy, for different types of tension, to prevent them from getting mixed up.

Tamara has not said anything yet.

"But we already have so many meetings. If there's one thing I really don't want it's more meetings. They take too long and I always have a hard time paying attention throughout them."

Neil is about to jump in to defend their team meeting, when John responds. "Holacracy does have meetings; that's true. But the meetings are short and disciplined. It cuts out all the noise that often characterizes meetings. But that's not all. Because you make clear, explicit agreements, you waste far less time on follow-up and one-on-one's to get aligned, on little irritations that you have to resolve, on emails CC-ing everyone in the team. Instead, you just get on with your work and stay focused. Ultimately, you end up *saving* time. There are a number of default roles in Holacracy that ensure that meetings don't get out of hand. The most important one is the role of the Facilitator, who leads the meetings and enforces the rules of the game."

"You mean Neil?"

"No, I mean the Facilitator, which can be anyone except the manager. I'll get back to that after the break."

Neil takes a deep breath. He's not sure how he feels about all of this.

○

During the break, Neil confronts John.

"What did you mean when you were talking about this

Facilitator role? Who is going to be leading the meetings?"

"The team elects its own Facilitator."

"Interesting."

"I can see you're struggling with that."

"Well, I just don't see who in the team should be the Facilitator then. Chairing meetings is an art. I'm not saying I'm great at it, but ..."

"You're getting ahead of yourself, Neil. You really don't have to worry about it yet. Initially, I will be the Facilitator."

"Hmm. Chairing meetings is part of my job. Every manager in this company chairs their own team meetings."

"Just to be honest, Neil, I have never attended one of your meetings, but from what I've been hearing from your team, it sounds like they're not going all that well. But you're no exception."

"Thanks," Neil says wryly.

"No problem." John smiles.

"Do you think we will get the team onboard?"

"Is that important to you?"

"Yes, it is."

"What will you do if they say no?"

"I don't know."

"See, you've kind of painted yourself into a corner, haven't you? You are the manager, and as far as I am aware, you want to do this."

"That's true."

"To give yourself some room, I would suggest that you bring this to the team as an experiment. A four-month experiment."

"I would not have thought of that."

"I know," John grins, "but I've been around the block a few times."

THE EXPERIMENT

When everyone has returned after the break, John gets back to what he was talking about. He tells the group more about how decision-making works in Holacracy's meetings.

"How many of you have ever attended a meeting where you didn't manage to get through all of the agenda points?"

They all raise their hands.

"Why do you think that happens?"

"Some people are just long-winded," Will calls out; he does his best not to look at Suzanne.

Suzanne adds, "And I think we talk too much about details. We hardly ever get to the strategic issues."

Lien offers, "We always want to hear everyone's opinion. And we keep going until everyone agrees."

"Ah! And what if I told you that that doesn't matter? That you can also make good decisions without everyone agreeing?"

Suzanne asks, "What on earth do you mean?"

"I'm talking about workable decisions. Sometimes you just have to decide that something is workable and then go on."

"That sounds a bit weak to me." Suzanne raises her voice just a little bit. "I don't know, but I think all of us here are pretty ambitious. I always shoot for the moon. No guts, no glory. What you're saying sounds very mediocre to me."

Neil can see the others nodding in agreement and fears that the mood is about to change. He quickly throws in a question. "Could you explain what it means to you for an idea to be workable?"

John takes a step forward.

"Let me turn the question around: when is a decision *not* workable?" Answers are called out immediately.

"If it's unclear what it means."

"Not feasible."

"Impractical."

John continues. "Okay; interesting. All true. In other words, if you'd all be worse off than you would be if you had never made that decision. Now, how about if I formulate it a bit differently: something is not workable if it's a step back or if it does harm." He looks at Tamara while he says it.

"Exactly! That reminds me of that IT project we did last year! What a disaster that was!"

"Okay, so not workable is clear?"

"It is to me," Tamara says, and the others nod.

"Well, now you also know when something *is* workable ... that is, if it's not a step back and doesn't do harm. Meaning it's good enough and safe enough to try."

Tamara's face brightens and the others nod in agreement.

Neil interjects, "But, wait a minute, John. How does this ensure that the meetings run faster?"

"The main thing is that you begin to use the idea of a workable decision as a basic principle. You can talk all you want and hear everyone's opinions, but in meetings, the most important thing is often helping the person who's stuck get unstuck. And if it's a decision that affects the whole team, you don't sit around and discuss it endlessly until you've made the perfect decision for everyone."

"That *would* save a lot of time," Lien says. The others nod affirmatively.

"Perfection is the enemy of good enough," Soraya notes wisely.

John confirms, "Exactly! Going for workable decisions is much smarter. Because if you decide that something is safe enough to try, then you can just go and do it."

John pauses for a moment to let his words sink in.

Suzanne is squirming in her chair. "But isn't that the mediocrity that I was mentioning earlier?"

John smiles. "I understand why you'd think that. Making workable decisions, by itself, is not enough. The other key piece here is continuous improvement. As soon as you move into action, you'll find out what works and what doesn't, and you can make adjustments. In this way, your workable solution becomes better and better as you go, rather than trying to design a perfect solution upfront and hoping for the best."

John prepares to complete his presentation.

Neil looks at his watch—another fifteen minutes. He senses that this is a good time to do a temperature check. John's presentation has certainly been very convincing to him. He stands up in front of the group and asks, "Well, what do you think? Is getting started with Holacracy 'workable' for you?" The way in which Neil slowly and clearly articulates the word, makes them laugh.

"What John told us really appeals to me, especially if it can help us save time," Soraya says. "I think this is really going to help us."

Will adds, "To be honest, I do have to admit that our current meeting style is not working. Even if all we accomplish is having more efficient meetings, that's a big plus."

Tamara is not convinced. "I'm not sure if I agree or not. I think it still involves a lot of meetings. I can relate to the part about tension. But I hate meetings and the last thing I need is more of them."

"What about you, Suzanne?" Neil asks.

"I'm still having my doubts. The autonomy definitely appeals to me. But on the other hand, I'm not really excited about new systems. In my experience, they never really improve anything. Plus, I'm afraid it will distract us from our work."

Tamara concurs. "Suzanne does have a point."

For a minute, Neil is afraid they'll descend back into a discussion. *Stay calm; not everyone has to agree.* "Let me put it another way: I am convinced. But I can understand people still feeling doubtful. I started to see the necessity of this when we got the North American deal. I don't want to force anything, but I'd like to ask you to take on this experiment together for the next four months."

"And if the experiment fails?" is Suzanne's laconic response.

Neil looks at John. "Can you speak to that, John?"

"The goal of your experiment is to find a new way of working. In that sense, it can't fail, because things will definitely change. Holacracy will also provide you with many opportunities to adjust things based on your day-to-day reality. That's pretty much built-in."

Suzanne says, "If the majority wants this, I'm not going to stand in the way. But I still have to see. I'm not going to change just for the sake of change. I've been there, and done that."

2.2 INTRODUCING HOLACRACY

In 2001, the American entrepreneur Brian Robertson co-founded the company Ternary Software. Just like Neil, he was convinced that things could be done differently, that you had to be able to make better use of the creativity, entrepreneurship, and engagement of the people you work with. He began to experiment with a range of ideas and methods. Ternary created its software according to the Agile method from the start, so everyone was used to that. Getting Things Done was also a revelation for Robertson: that kind of clarity and flow was something he wanted throughout the entire company!

Holacracy was developed from the belief that there must be a better way to run a company

It certainly wasn't easy, but after a few years, the experiment stabilized. And he called it "Holacracy," a combination of the word "holarchy" and the suffix "-cracy." A holarchy refers to a natural hierarchy, like, for example, a cell, which is made up of molecules, which in turn are made up of atoms. Or a sentence that is made up of words, which in turn are made up of letters. The suffix originates from the Greek *krateo* (κρατέω), which means "to govern" or "to steer." Instead of governance by the people, as in democracy, Holacracy refers to governance through a natural hierarchy, a form of self-organization.

Holacracy summarized

Holacracy is a way of organizing where you continuously adjust the structure based on tension. Such tension serves as fuel for constantly improving the way you work. It tells you where something is needed or something is going off-track. Or, as we saw earlier, where there is a gap between the current and the desired reality. Holacracy ensures that *every* tension becomes fuel for moving the team or organization forward towards its purpose.

Holacracy uses tension as fuel to improve the way you work

So what does that look like in practice? In Holacracy, everyone takes on one or more roles. The role describes exactly what is expected of you and what you have authority to make decisions about. Together, these roles form a "circle," which fulfills a specific purpose within the larger organization.

Usually we just call this a team, so what exactly is the difference between a team and a circle? A team is made up of people, and a circle is made up of roles. In a circle, the focus is not on the people, but rather on the work that they do and the roles they fill. These roles are determined by the circle itself, in regular 'governance meetings'.

In Holacracy, everyone fills one or more roles

In addition to governance meetings, each circle also has 'tactical meetings', which focus on the day-to-day work of the circle. These are two very different meetings that often get mixed up. Just separating these two conversations already creates much more clarity.

Clarity and flow

The tactical meeting and the governance meeting each have their own rules. These rules ensure crisp and effective meetings, focused on the circle's purpose; the work it does, the function it fulfills for the larger organization. These meetings require a lot of discipline and result in little room for noise and friction. Everyone knows exactly what is expected of them.

Each circle has regular tactical and governance meetings, which each have their own rules

When you fill a role, it's up to you how you want to get the work done. If you run into a tension or an obstacle, you bring it up at the next tactical meeting. If something's off in the way the circle functions or in our expectations of roles, you can bring a proposal to the next governance meeting. In this way, Holacracy creates ever-more clarity, so that the circle can get and stay "in flow."

2.3 TENSION IS FUEL

Holacracy is all about tension. Good for Neil and his team, because with the pressure from the new campaign, there's no shortage of tension! So far though, they're having a bit of a hard time dealing with it in a constructive way. Instead, it has been leading to frustration and conflict, because everyone has a slightly different perspective. Could Holacracy help?

You can't understand Holacracy without understanding the concept of a tension. Tension is reality telling you: this is how it is *now*—and this is how it *could* be done. This gap between how it is and how it could is sometimes called creative tension. It doesn't always feel particularly 'creative' though. In fact, whether you experience a tension as negative or positive depends on how you look at it. If you say, "This is how it is, but this is how it *should* be," then you are probably experiencing the tension as something negative, as a problem. If you say, "This is how it is, and this is how it *could* be," you are seeing it more as an opportunity, as something positive. Tension only gets a positive or negative charge when you "label" it. Without a label, tension is neutral—it's just information.

Tension is how reality gives you feedback; it offers information about how things are and how they could be or should be

Wasting energy

If you don't know how to deal with tension, you can waste a lot of energy. Instead of treating tension as information, team members try to convince each other about their point of view, for example on whether it is a problem or an opportunity. Or maybe you argue about whether the tension someone is sensing is even "true" or "right"! In some teams, everyone has to agree before anything happens. In other teams, the leader in particular has to "get it" and make a decision. Sometimes people take a tension personally, leading them to get stressed out or defensive. Or you can always sweep a tension under the carpet. These are all different ways of "wasting" tension.

Use every bit of tension

Tension is energy, just like the charge that's created by two magnetic poles. If you have to argue about every tension or if you immediately sweep it under the rug, you're not using this energy very productively. But you can also use tension to change something or put something into motion! Just as in physics, the law of conservation of energy applies: tension can never be truly lost; it can only change forms. If you don't do something with a tension, it will reappear in a different form, for example, as frustration or resistance. Or by blowing off steam at home. Or instead, you can use this energy as fuel for change. In fact, the promise of Holacracy is using *every* tension as fuel, no matter where the tension is picked up or by whom. If you can accomplish that, you will truly have a "learning organization"!

Tension can morph into resistance, frustration, or friction. But you can also use the energy as fuel for change.

Everyone is a sensor

Everyone is effectively a sensor that is constantly picking up tension. No two people are the same; every sensor senses at a slightly different wavelength and so brings in a unique perspective. To argue whether a particular kind of tension is "true" or not is about as useful as a discussion about the "right" temperature in the house. They are both subjective experiences. Instead of arguing about this, you want to *use* those different perspectives, by learning something from it or by making a change. Tension is then no longer "sand in the machine," but the fuel it runs on.

Everyone is a unique sensor that is constantly sensing tension

THE BOSS

The next morning, Neil is reading his mail. There is a proposal from John for his consulting fee. Neil isn't happy with how the session ended yesterday. He knows that if Suzanne is not on board he can expect opposition from her down the road. He doesn't want to take that chance. He has seen her rebelliousness in action in the past. It's nice, this idea of making workable decisions, but it doesn't give him any certainty. It it just John's lingo that he needs to get used to? He looks back at the last few months: the painful meetings, the tensions. Time is of the essence; he can't take forever to figure this out. He looks at the proposal again. He would prefer to get Rakesh's approval; he's spoken about it with him before. When he walks into Rakesh's office, he finds him squinting his eyes at his computer screen. He is concentrating so hard he barely even notices Neil walking into his office, until he's right by his desk.

"Oh, it's you. How's the campaign coming?"

"We're working on it ..."

"Do you need me to sign something?"

"A proposal. We discussed it a while back. I'd like to hire someone to help me make my team more productive."

"This Hola something?"

"Holacracy."

"Right, Holocracy. I assume you have given this some thought?"

"We had a session about it with the whole team yesterday."

"And did everyone get on board?"

"Almost everyone."

"Almost?"

"Suzanne's having her doubts."

"Are you sure you want to move forward then?" Rakesh looks at the proposal. "Okay, I'll sign it, but you're going to have to deliver the result."

"It's not going to be easy, but I see an opportunity to take my team to the next level with this campaign."

"All right, it's your team. You're the one that has to deal with Suzanne. And even if she's not excited about this, you're the boss. You evaluate her performance, not the other way around. ... Just as I evaluate yours."

"Understood."

Back at his desk, Neil immediately schedules a kick-off meeting for the implementation with John in three days.

THE RULES

The office at Qwest Plaza has had a lot of residents over the years, and all of them have left their mark. The conference room they've taken over was last used as a boardroom. The last tenant, an ad agency, left big design lamps behind on the ceiling. Neil shows John the boardroom. He is impressed with the space and the view.

"Great you were available so soon," Neil says.

"Yes, it's nice to have a client here at home. I'm tired of traveling for a while."

"I spoke with my boss and he supports the process."

"Great."

"You talk about clarity a lot; I think that's what's lacking in this team."

John nods.

"You might have got the impression that I don't make decisions, that I want everyone to agree."

"That sure didn't work in the last session," John points out.

"This afternoon, I want to make it perfectly clear to the team that I have the final say in this."

"Right now, that is exactly what you need to do. In fact, I will explicitly ask you to sign the Holacracy Constitution today," John says.

Before Neil can ask John about this constitution, the team files into the boardroom. John waits until everyone has their coffee and they're all in their chairs before he opens the session. He introduces his implementation approach, which will take four months.

Suzanne interrupts him almost immediately. "Whoa, wait a

minute! This is moving along very fast. I missed the decision to go ahead with this. Last time I said that I was willing to try it and now we're already talking about an implementation plan."

Neil tells her, "I have decided we are going to do this. I took your opinion into consideration, as well as the fact that the majority wants this. Ultimately, I went ahead and made the decision."

"I think it would have been more polite to involve everyone in the decision," Suzanne says.

Will speaks up."I'm glad Neil made the decision. Now we all know where we stand."

Neil is surprised with this show of support from an unexpected quarter.

Suzanne isn't done. "Making the decision together creates much more ownership."

"That may be," Neil responds, "but I think for us that has gotten out of hand. We have too many meetings about everything under the sun and they are all far too long."

John cuts the discussion short: "I see that there are different ideas here about the authority to make decisions. Suzanne, you want everyone to decide, while Neil and Will want the manager to make decisions."

Neil asks, "Isn't it Holacracy's job to make that clear? If you're the manager, then that means you make the final decision."

"Well, not exactly," John explains. "What Holacracy does, is distribute authority into well-defined roles, so there is no longer a single manager that makes decisions for the whole team."

Suzanne nods. "Sounds more like what I was talking about."

"But it's not like everyone decides about everything together either," John continues. "That's different. Making decisions is about exercising your authority. We will begin to make this very explicit by setting up clear roles, each with their own area or accountability and authority. The rules for how that all works exactly are in the Holacracy Constitution."

John picks up a book from the table and holds it up. "Everything you want to know about decision-making and authority in Holacracy, you can find in here."

Tamara looks pained. "Hey, we're not going to regulate everything to death, are we?"

John smiles. "Well, that's certainly not the plan. These rules just ensure that we can play the game. Just like soccer, for example. No rules, no game."

John holds up a onepager. "

the first step in adopting Holacracy is for the existing power-holder to sign the Constitution. By signing this, he distributes his authority."

Neil looks startled. "What do you mean, John ... distribute authority?"

"Right now, you have exclusive authority to decide how works gets done in the team, and when you sign this document, you distribute that authority."

"To whom?"

"To a well-defined process, which you will use to decide who does what and how you work together as a team."

Neil sighs. "Do I really have to sign this? It's just a formality, isn't it?"

"Actually," John explains, "it's more than a formality. This is where we agree on the new rules of the game, and by signing this you agree that no one is above those rules, not even you as the manager."

Neil can see that John really means it. "You're not making this easy for me."

"If you want this to work ..."

For a moment it is completely quiet. Then Neil gets up, walks up and puts his signature under the Holacracy Constitution.

○

Neil is experiencing conflicting feelings. During the days that follow, he finds himself repeatedly wondering what his signature really means. He finds it hard to see what it will mean in terms of his authority within the team.

After the boardroom session, John gave the team some homework. Everyone had to keep track of what it is they do day-by-day, at least for a while. John had been very specific about this, so Neil was also keeping track of everything he did. He had thought it would be easy enough, but he actually found it quite challenging to be honest and track exactly what he was doing. The insight into how he actually spent his time was pretty confronting at times; he had not realized how much time he spent on relatively unimportant things!

When he phones John a few days later, he feels the uncertainty still gnawing at him.

"Am I going to make myself redundant?"

John laughs. "You're afraid you won't have anything left to do?"

"Maybe. As the manager, you're there to solve people's problems and chase them so they don't forget anything. I've gotten pretty good at that, because I still need to jump in regularly. For example, the other day I decided to cancel a mailing because there was an error in it."

"Is that how you look at your role as a manager?"

"If I don't keep an eye on it all, things are guaranteed to get derailed."

"So, you are saying that the team needs you to solve problems that they can't solve themselves?"

"Yes, basically."

"That sounds like it takes up a lot of time and energy. How many hours a week do you work?"

"Up to sixty, sometimes."

"And how does your wife feel about that?"

"She's not too happy about it," Neil says.

"I can understand that. Anyway, you're not the only one. I did the same thing for years myself. I was president of a company, and whenever there were any problems, everyone would come running to me to solve it. I got very good at it. I thought I was a pretty tough guy when I told everyone how demanding my work was and how hard I worked." John goes quiet for a moment.

"The result was that I got burned out and ended up having to take a six-month leave just to recover from the stress. That's when someone explained to me what I had been doing to myself. 'Heroic leadership is what you call that,' he said. And that's what you're doing now. You believe you're the one that has to keep the ship afloat. And you get a big kick every time you save the day, adrenaline coursing through your veins; it feels great, doesn't it? You could get addicted to that feeling. But the effect is actually the opposite."

"What do you mean?"

"This heroic leadership style prevents your team members from feeling accountable and taking ownership themselves. Whenever something goes wrong, there's always you to fix it. None of you want it, but that's what inevitably happens."

"So how is distributing my authority going to help with that?"

"You make it clear that from now on, it's no longer about you. Instead, you will have to work together, using Holacracy's rules and processes to create clarity and take ownership, with everyone leading their own roles."

"Sounds great, rules and processes, but can we really trust it to work?"

"How long can you go on being the heroic leader? You can't afford to be the bottleneck in your team. Distributing authority and playing by the same rules is a lot more effective, and a lot more reliable than what you're doing now.

"Are you saying that leadership is not needed anymore?"

"No, in fact I'm saying the opposite. Distributed leadership means *everyone* shows leadership, within their own roles and accountabilities."

"That sounds to me like it's going a bit far. All the management books I read talk about inspiring leaders who transform their organizations."

"And there is nothing wrong with that. In conventional organizations, it's important to have leaders that can create change. But let me ask you something. You know the theories, you have the skills, and you work sixty hours a week. So why haven't you succeeded with your team?"

Neil is thoughtful. "Maybe it's me ... maybe I need to work more on my leadership style?"

"It certainly can't do any harm to look at yourself with a critical eye, but don't underestimate the effect of your environment and the systems and structures you work in."

Neil nods. "I get that. You mean the 'operating system' that you keep talking about?"

"Exactly. You can work on your leadership style or send everyone on another training, but ultimately the game won't change until you change the rules. So now that we've done that, it's time to get out onto the field and learn to play this new game. Are you ready for that?"

"I think so," Neil says.

2.4 IMPLEMENTING HOLACRACY

Starting something new is always exciting. This is the time to get clear about what you are going to do and what results you want. At the same time, you're not exactly sure what you're getting yourself into. Neil wonders if Holacracy is really going to solve his problem, and what his role will be. What has he started, exactly?

Getting started with Holacracy

Holacracy is not an update; it is an entirely new operating system for your team or organization. It requires a new language, unlearning old behavior, and learning new behavior. The way in which decisions are made will undergo a major transformation. In Holacracy, the manager gets a different role. It is, in fact, a whole new way of thinking, just like with Getting Things Done. For the sake of convenience, we will call this process an "implementation." That sounds nice and tangible. At the same time, it is a bit of a risky word, because it creates the impression that Holacracy is a ready-made solution you can just "roll out." In reality though, the key lies in changing the way the team thinks and works. And that is not something you can just "implement."

The goal

You most likely have a good reason to want to explore Holacracy. What are the challenges and questions that keep coming back? What are the issues you can't resolve with a simple project or a workshop? These are the tensions that serve as fuel for implementing Holacracy. For Neil and his team, these include:

- Lack of clarity regarding accountabilities and conflicting expectations
- Ineffective decision-making and painful meetings
- Lack of prioritization and conscious choices, resulting in stress and conflict

These are not random problems; they are symptoms. They are the natural consequences of the way the team currently functions. Unintended consequences, no doubt, but unfortunately, also unavoidable. As they say in the software world: they're features, not bugs. In other words: they are not errors in the system, they are part of the design! In order to change this, the system as a whole needs to change.

The problems that teams and organizations wrestle with are not random; they are the unavoidable consequences of the way they are set up

And that is the purpose of a Holacracy implementation: to create a clear and organic structure within which the work is carried out in a natural and smooth way. As you have seen by now, this structure is not designed upfront. We are going to develop it organically and then adjust things step by step, based on the tensions that will inevitably show up.

The Holacracy Constitution

The rules of Holacracy are spelled out exactly in the Holacracy Constitution. For example, the constitution states what rights and obligations you have as a member of a circle. You could compare it to the rules of a game, like soccer or chess. While you're play-ing you probably won't need to look at these rules, but you know you can always refer back to them in the event of any lack of clar-ity or a conflict. This is how Holacracy works too: when you get stuck, or if something is unclear, you can refer to the constitution. You formally adopt the Holacracy Constitution by having the cur-rent power-holder (most often the manager) sign it. After that they will be in effect and they apply to everyone, including the manag-er him or herself!

The implementation process

The implementation process of Holacracy has four steps, which correspond with the following four chapters of this book:

1. Describing and assigning the initial roles (Chapter 3)
2. Starting up the governance meetings (Chapter 4)
3. Working within the roles (Chapter 5)
4. Starting up the tactical meetings (Chapter 6)

Our first step is to describe the initial roles, based on the current reality. These will be adjusted at regular governance meetings, based on tensions. In parallel, we kick off the week-ly tactical meetings, in which the focus lies not on the roles, but on the work itself. During day-to-day work, lots of tensions will show up, and we will use these tensions to further evolve the roles. The duration of the implementation depends primarily on the frequency of these tactical and governance meetings.

Governance meetings don't happen every week, like the tac-tical meetings, but every two weeks. Once there's some momen-tum, the governance meetings generally happen once a month. All in all, it takes several months before everything is running smoothly. It is highly recommended that these meetings are initially led by someone who already knows the game (the Facilitator role). If you don't, you risk never escaping the "gravitational pull" of old patterns of behavior. The goal, of course, is for the circle to become self-sufficient. On average, it takes about three to six months to really learn Holacracy. You could also say that that's just the beginning: after all, there's no finish line for evolution!

An average Holacracy implementation takes three to six months

THREE

ROLES AND ACCOUNTABILITIES

THE ROLES

When Neil enters the boardroom, he notices that it is set up differently. The chairs and the table have been pushed to the side and a large space has been cleared in front of the whiteboard. There are stacks of Post-its and markers everywhere. He is not sure what to expect.

"Weren't we going to talk about filling the positions today?"

"We're going to be talking about roles and accountabilities."

"Oh, then I have to go out for a minute."

"All right, we'll be starting in five minutes."

Neil walks back to his desk and gets the file with all the job descriptions out of the filing cabinet. This is a good opportunity to finally complete those profiles; something he's been wanting to do for ages. John waits until everyone has come in. A few minutes later, the group is standing in a circle around the whiteboard.

"Well, did everyone do their homework?"

"Yes, sir," Tamara grins.

"And how did it go?"

"It was much harder than I had thought to come up with that list of activities you wanted us to make," Will says. "I thought I had everything pretty well organized, but the things I have on my list now are different from the ones I had in my head."

"Excellent," John responds. "Well done. The next step is for each of you to go to the board, one by one, and stick a note on it for every activity."

Lien is the first one to go to the board, and she starts to stick notes onto it.

"Oh, and try to cluster related activities together, while you're at it," John says.

Gradually the board gets filled up with Post-its. Neil is surprised at what he sees appearing on the board. He grabs his job descriptions and takes some notes. John notices Neil writing.

"Well, what does it look like? Does it match?"

"No, not really. But it's interesting. I'm writing this down so that I can update our job descriptions."

"We'll get back to that a bit later," John says. He asks the team to finalize the clusters of activities. All of them are at the board now, putting up notes and moving them around. It takes a while, but at last all the Post-its are divided into groups.

"And now it's time to name each cluster."

There is a bit of discussion, but finally all the clusters have a descriptive label.

"Okay. So these are the initial roles: our point of departure."

Neil says, "You mean the positions."

"No, I mean the roles," John replies. "The descriptions are probably incomplete at this point, but this is a reasonable description of the work you are all doing *now*. So, these are the initial roles."

Neil sits down and takes a deep breath. It feels a bit odd to have everyone talking about things that he usually thinks about by himself, or that he discusses only with Human Resources. The department's organizational chart is on the table in front of him.

"I'm seeing a lot of similarities with how we already work now. As well as things that are different. It looks like a good inventory to me. But, in practical terms, couldn't we adjust the existing job titles to match this inventory we just created?"

"I wouldn't recommend doing that, Neil. Of course, we don't

expect this to be completely different from the existing jobs being done. But the point here is that this is an organic structure that comes directly from your actual day-to-day activities; it is not made up or designed," John says emphatically.

Neil looks at his org chart again.

"So much work has already been done on this in the past. It seems like a waste not to use it at all. And I don't think we have the time to create a whole new structure. That would be foolish, wouldn't it? Since we have so much already?"

Soraya supports John, saying, "With all due respect, those job descriptions you're talking about? I don't even know what's in those. I can relate to what's on the board."

Neil is starting to feel uncomfortable; Soraya usually agrees with him.

"I've never even looked at mine," Lien says.

Neil is tempted to reply to that, but he manages to swallow it.

John closes the matter. "Listen you guys, today is not the day we are going to design the perfect structure. This is just our point of departure. If we tried to get it exactly right, we would soon get lost in the details."

○

Neil had not expected Soraya and Lien to be so critical of his job descriptions. He had worked really hard on them. He waits until everyone has left the room.

John looks at him. "What's bothering you?"

"How are we supposed to go ahead with a half-finished structure? I feel like we are further from our goal instead of closer."

"We've created the foundation for the first governance meeting."

"Do I still have any kind of authority? Or have I distributed everything?"

"Of course you still have some authority and, in fact, that is a very important point." John grabs the constitution from his bag and opens it to a page that reads LEAD LINK across the top. He offers it to Neil without saying anything, As Neil reads what it says, his anxiety begins to subside and he gradually feels like he can relax again.

"So I'm the Lead Link?"

"You fill the role of Lead Link."

"Filling a role—what's the difference compared to what I do now?" A note of impatience is starting to creep into Neil's voice.

"You are not your role. The role is an organizational unit that someone energizes. Let me put it another way: You are the Marketing Director here, right?"

"Yes, I am."

"Did you notice that? You're saying 'I am.' But what if I told you the Marketing Director is underperforming?"

That startles Neil. "What do you mean?"

"I can tell that startled you. That's what happens when you identify with a label. It makes you take things personally."

"But that's only natural, isn't it?"

"It is understandable, but that doesn't mean it's natural. If you take things personally, you fail to distinguish between your own needs and the needs of the organization. Then things get mixed up and you start to relate the tension to yourself in a personal way. Which means you then have to deal with ego and politics."

John thumbs through the document.

"Back to the Lead Link: It is one of the core roles that every circle has. These core roles have a number of default accountabilities. For example, you, as the Lead Link, have the authority to assign roles to people. And before we have the first governance meetings, you need to assign the roles we created today. Now, are you ready to step into your new role as the Lead Link?"

"It sounds less sexy than Marketing Director, but, okay. We'll see how it goes."

3.1 THE MISSING LINK

The first step in implementing Holacracy is to map out the roles in the team. Neil is struggling; did he write those job descriptions for nothing? And is this really going to help increase the team's productivity? Why are those roles so important?

The bridge between two worlds

Roles are the link between the day-to-day work and the overall goals. Most people prefer one over the other. Some of us most enjoy taking concrete action to find out what works and what doesn't. Others prefer to take a step back to clarify what the goal is and how best to approach it. When that link between the day-to-day work and the goal is missing, then there are two separate worlds. One is the world of the day-to-day reality and the operational issues that keep you busy. This is where the visible work is done and you are firmly rooted in everyday reality. The other world is that of goals and desired outcomes. This is the desired reality, which is not nearly as visible. By taking a step back from the issues of the day, you can distinguish the forest from the trees.

Roles are the link between the day-to-day reality and the desired reality

When that link is missing, you won't get far: if you don't know where you're supposed to get to, hard work doesn't help. Conversely, no matter how well you know what the goal is, if you don't translate it into tangible action steps, you won't ever see those ideas become reality.

Roles and accountabilities

The only way to connect these two worlds to each other is by creating a link between the day-to-day work and the desired reality. This doesn't just apply to the team; your own everyday work also needs to be connected to your goals. When it isn't, that creates lots of tension. This is where roles and accountabilities come into play. The way we use the term here, a role refers to a collection of accountabilities that naturally belong together. Accountabilities refer to areas or activities that you need to pay attention to continuously to achieve your goals.

A role consists of accountabilities, which each refer to an area or activity that you need to pay attention to in order to reach your goals

An example of a role with accountabilities is that of a "parent," who is accountable for raising the children and creating a safe environment for them to grow up in. And maybe the same person also fills the role of "HR Manager," accountable for recruiting and selecting employees and developing HR policies. As you can see, a person can fill many roles in life and work.

Areas of focus

In contrast to projects or actions, accountabilities are never "finished". Most of your everyday work results directly from accountabilities that are related to one or more roles. In some cases these are implicit and you rarely think about them (the role of "parent," for example), while others are very explicit ("Marketing Director"). Remember the image of the bridge between two worlds? Do you ever feel that your everyday work is not (sufficiently) connected to your goals? Then it is likely that you do not have enough clarity about the areas of focus in your work or in your life: your roles and accountabilities. Or maybe you've got your own roles mapped out, but it's the *division* of roles (for example, within your team, or in your marriage) that is not clear. In that case, a lot can be gained by getting crystal-clear on this. And the good news is that it's not that difficult!

3.2 MAKING EXPECTATIONS EXPLICIT

Roles are at the heart of Holacracy. They not only connect the everyday reality to the desired reality, but they also connect the organization to the people that work there. The roles you fulfill determine what exactly is expected of you.

Roles are the connection between the organization and the people that work there

That's probably why we tend to get so obsessed with titles: the greater the expectations, the more important you appear to be. We expect more from a manager than we do from a clerk, whether or not the title of 'manager' is preceded by the labels "logistics," "helpdesk," or "financial." But in practice, those expectations turn out to be not that clear. What exactly are you accountable for? What exactly can I count on you for? And what authority do you have to make decisions? Ask three colleagues and you will get three different answers—and all of them will be different again from the formal job description.

Accountability and authority

Different expectations: they are the source of nearly every conflict in the workplace. As long as people's expectations are not clear, these conflicts will often feel like personal conflicts. But in reality, the conflicts are usually not about the individuals, but about the roles involved; they are role conflicts.

The vast majority of conflicts at work are, in fact, role conflicts

The purpose of the roles in Holacracy is to make the expectations explicit in order to create clarity around them. With roles, you can accurately describe what you can and cannot expect from each other. You do this by defining exactly what activities a role is accountable for, for example, the Database role, which has "Backing up the database regularly" as one of its accountabilities. If this is one of the roles you fill, others can count on you for doing that; they can hold you accountable. Of course, you also need to have the relevant authority, so that you can make decisions about how to best energize a specific accountability. Holacracy therefore automatically couples authority with accountability. Roles are like "blood vessels", through which accountability and authority are distributed throughout the organization. In Holacracy terms, this is called "distributed authority", and it is a radical departure from the traditional management hierarchy, where authority is concentrated in one or a few individuals who (can) make all the decisions.

Roles make expectations explicit and define accountability and authority

What that means, is that in Holacracy, you are not a 'cog in the wheel'; you are an entrepreneur in your roles, with real accountability *and* authority to make decisions.

Roles versus positions

At first glance, a role appears similar to a position. A job description often includes responsibilities and authorities, after all. However, there are a few important differences. First of all, positions are carefully designed upfront and mostly static. Of course, they could be adjusted occasionally, but this rarely happens. A role description, on the other hand, is constantly evolving on the basis of tensions. Moreover, roles are not designed by someone from Human Resources or by some consultant, but by the circle in which the role lives. They are based on what is happening on the ground, rather than on some theory or analysis of how it should or could be. Finally, roles are much more flexible and "fluid" than a position. A role is often smaller than a position; most people therefore fill multiple roles. All in all, you can look at roles as a sort of "Agile version" of positions.

Roles are defined by the circle itself and are continuously adjusted, whereas positions are designed outside the circle and are static

3.3 DEFINING THE INITIAL ROLES

If roles, unlike positions, are not designed by Human Resources or a consultant, how are they created? And what do you do with existing job descriptions, like the ones Neil had created in the past? The short answer is: you are going to describe them, based on the current reality. This means that we are consciously putting aside any existing descriptions of roles or positions. Instead, we are going to look carefully at who does what *now*. This is what John asked the team members to do—to keep track of exactly what they do day to day, at least for a while.

Current reality as the point of departure

That sounds easy—perhaps even too easy? It certainly isn't complicated, but you have to watch out for a few things. The main thing is to start with the *current* reality and not with how you think it could or should be. The roles will be adjusted regularly in the circle's governance meetings, so you don't need more than a starting point. The current situation offers the best point of departure, because from here you can start evolving roles based on actual tensions, instead of assumptions and predictions.

When describing the circle's initial roles, start with the current reality; not with how you think it could or should be

The easiest way to create that point of departure is by keeping track of what everyone does day to day, for some specified amount of time—not what you would have liked to do, or what you should have done, but what you actually did. If you do this for a few weeks, at some point you will begin to see a pattern. Hidden in your list of day to day work, you will find a number of ongoing or recurring activities. Those activities are the ones we will use as the foundation for defining the initial roles and accountabilities.

Good enough

After everyone has kept track of what they do day to day for a few weeks, it is time to share the results with the circle. This should give you a pretty good overview of the activities of the circle as a whole. We will create the first version of the roles based on this overview. It does not need to be more than a starting point, because reality will be giving us feedback in the form of tensions! These tensions are the fuel we will use to evolve our roles and accountabilities in the circle's governance meetings. Because you are never finished with this and the role structure is never "done," "good enough" is more than sufficient as a starting point.

> The first roles do not need to be complete or perfect; after all, we will be adjusting them continuously, based on actual tensions sensed by circle members

3.4 KEEPING TRACK OF YOUR DAILY ACTIVITIES

Before the initial roles can be defined, some individual preparation is required by each member of the circle. The objective is to get an overview of everyone's various activities. The main pitfall is to make up what you should or could do, instead of describing what you actually do each day. It is helpful to take at least two or three weeks to track exactly what you do day to day. You can track this on a list or in your calendar, or you can use an online service which sends you a daily reminder email and records your activities on a simple calendar.

What did I do today?

What it comes down to is that at the end of every work day, you answer the question, "What did I do today?" Not "What would I have liked to do?" or "What should I *really* have done?" but what you actually did. If your work is routine, one week might be enough. But if your work is varied, you might need to keep your list for a bit longer to get a clear picture.

> *Keep track of what you do each day for several weeks; not what you would have liked to do or should have done, but what you actually did each day*

Don't forget: the overview does not have to be "complete";

for now we are just looking for "good enough." The main thing is get an overview of your work, so you can identify your *ongoing* activities.

Here is an example of a number of things that could be on Neil's list at the end of the day:

- Prepared presentation for management
- Meeting with Soraya about monthly report
- Submitted budget for Q3
- Updated declarations
- Read research report
- Spoke with Denis on the phone about campaign's progress
- Meeting with Tamara about client mailing
- Prepared performance meeting with Lien

You don't need to record every little task and phone call. What we are looking for is an overview of your main activities. Some days you may have three or four, other days ten. But if you have twenty every day, you are probably getting caught up in too much detail. When you're satisfied with the list you have created, we go on to the next step.

Ongoing activities

Take your list and group the activities. Which ones belong together? What patterns do you see? Focus on the nature of the work and not too much on the exact content. The projects you work on change every few weeks or months, but the type of activities you do are often a lot less variable. Now, using this long list of grouped activities, we are going to scale it back to a shorter list of ongoing activities. The way we use the term here, an "ongoing activity" is more general than an action or a task. In addition, an ongoing activity, unlike actions and tasks, is never finished. Examples of Neil's ongoing activities are:

- Creating and monitoring budgets
- Developing strategy and annual plan
- Evaluating employees
- Conducting job interviews
- Maintaining contact with existing clients
- Reporting sales and marketing data to management

As you can see, each activity starts with a verb. This is no coincidence, because these verbs describe the nature of the activity. "Budgets" is not an activity, but "Creating and monitoring budgets" is. The "-ing" verbs describe activities that are ongoing, like "maintaining," "developing," "organizing," and so on. Verbs that describe visible, physical actions are usually too concrete and specific (e.g. "emailing", "speaking to", "calling", etc.). These are most often actions that have a more general, ongoing activity that drives them.

Group your daily activities and identify your ongoing activities, each with one or more clear "-ing" verbs that describe the activity

The line between actions and activities is often blurry. For example, you could say that "Conducting job interviews" refers to a recurring action.In this example, it may be such an important activity, which is happening on an ongoing basis, that it is counted as an ongoing activity. You should be able to come up with an average of five to ten ongoing activities from your list. If there are fewer, you have probably made it too generic. If there are (many) more, that is usually an indication that you are too caught up in the details, at least for this phase. There will be plenty of opportunity during the circle's governance meetings to add things and make them more specific!

3.5 FORMULATING ACCOUNTABILITIES AND ROLES

"So, did everyone do their homework?" John asks at the beginning of the meeting about roles. As it happens, everyone did keep track of what they did every day for several weeks. Based on this, they each created a list of their ongoing activities, an average of five to ten per person. Together, these activities provide a pretty good overview of the work being done by the circle as a whole. Now it's time for the next step: formulating the accountabilities and roles as a starting point for the first governance meeting.

Organic structure

It is very important to have the whole circle together to create the initial set of roles and accountabilities. It helps a lot if everyone writes down their ongoing activities on Post-it notes beforehand, clearly legible, one activity per note.

Make sure you have at least two hours available and that you have a room with a big empty surface, like a table, a wall or some large windows.

The ingredients for a work session about the initial roles: gather the entire circle in a room with a large, empty wall, plus a few pads of Post-it notes, for two hours!

The purpose of the work session is to stick all the notes onto the wall and cluster them. You can do this in two ways: everyone at once, in silence, or one at a time, with brief explanations from each person. The rest of the team listens and asks questions if something is not clear. Discussing too many details is the main pitfall here. Remember to stick to "good enough" for now and don't take too long for this step! Do not stick up the notes randomly; begin to cluster them right away. When the first person is finished, the next one can come forward with his or her notes. Where possible, add to the clusters that are already there. If you have a new and unrelated activity, start a new cluster. Continue until all the notes are on the wall, in clear clusters of ongoing activities. For this exercise, it is not important who put up which note or who is accountable for a specific activity at this time. We are looking for the organic structure in the current work of the circle. Which activities naturally belong together? Where does the work "live"? The point is that you are not looking at the people doing the work, but at the structure of the work itself.

When clustering activities, look for the organic structure in the work of the circle

If a lot of notes end up in one spot, see if you can divide that cluster into two or more new clusters in a natural way. You might end up with the odd activity that doesn't belong with anything else; treat these as separate clusters. You will see that as you continue to stick up notes, there will be more and more overlap between the activities in a cluster. This is perfectly normal; it means you are on the right track!

Assigning the initial roles

The clusters of ongoing activities are the foundation for the circle's initial roles. A role consists of one or more accountabilities. In Holacracy, an accountability is defined as an ongoing activity that the role is accountable for. This means that we are nearly there: the ongoing activities in each cluster are, in principle, the accountabilities of a role!

A role consists of one or more accountabilities, each of which refers to an ongoing activity that the role is accountable for

To convert the clusters of activities into roles and accountabilities, there are just two things left to do:

1. Summarize the (partially overlapping) activities into a number of clear accountabilities, and
2. Give each role a name.

It is easiest to start with step 2. When naming the roles, the focus should be on the content of the role. It's not about coming up with extravagant job titles (CEO, VP of Office Supplies, etc.), but about a role name that covers the accountabilities of the role. The name of the role is just a label; the accountabilities are what define exactly what a role is accountable for. Neil's team, for example, comes up with role names like Campaign, Online, Copywriter, Event Coordinator, PR, and Sales. The clearer the better!

The name of a role is just a label for the accountabilities that come with it

The exact formulation of each role's accountabilities may require a bit more attention (step 1). It is recommended to have one person figure this out after the work session, instead of having an endless group discussion about this. The main thing is that each accountability starts with a clear verb and that they all refer to an ongoing activity. You can easily check this: if you can complete the activity, then it is not ongoing. These activities are usually related to a project or a task. "Creating the budget for Q3" is not an ongoing activity; "Creating and monitoring budgets" is because it keeps coming back. Here is an example of a role Neil's team comes up with:

Campaign role – accountable for:
- Creating and maintaining campaign plans
- Briefing ad agencies for campaigns
- Testing campaigns
- Maintaining relationships with ad agencies

As you can see, each accountability starts with a verb. These are all accountabilities that you are never finished with; they are continuous activities. Incidentally, this is not completely black and white: there is no activity that goes on forever. So it is relative, but if you expect that in a few months or the next year, the activity will still be needed, we can call it continuous and give it a place among the roles of the circle.

Every accountability starts with a verb and refers to an ongoing activity

Some pitfalls and things to keep in mind

You can do this exercise with all kinds of different teams, and the amazing thing is that it always works! There are a few things you really have to watch out for, however. The main pitfall is the tendency to get lured away from the current reality. That's when you lose your grip on reality and end up on the slippery slope of wishes, opinions, and ideas (about how it could or should be done, for instance). In this exercise, you are looking for the organic structure of the circle, not for each team member's personal preferences. It is important to stay alert to this, because wishful thinking is a wobbly foundation for real change.

The second pitfall is to want to be complete. This shifts the attention from the key elements and moving parts to side issues and details. There is a good chance that trying to be complete will make you lose sight of the current reality. If, in two hours, you have captured most of the current activities in roles and accountabilities, that's more than enough. After all, the roles are nothing more than the starting point for continuous evolution, based on tensions and new data.

The third common pitfall is putting the focus on "who" instead of "what." In this exercise, it doesn't matter who put up which note, or even who is doing what. What matters is that you map out the circle's work and what does or does not belong together. The discussion about who fulfills which role is important, but separate from defining the roles in the first place. Questions about this should be saved until it is clear what roles and accountabilities there actually are.

The final pitfall is a lack of clarity about the activities. This is often related to formulation. As we saw earlier, "Budgets" is not an activity; "Creating and monitoring budgets" is.

The greatest pitfalls in creating the initial roles are wishful thinking, perfectionism, and a focus on "who" instead of "what"

3.6 ASSIGNING ROLES

After the work session with the circle, you now have a set of initial roles and accountabilities. It is almost time to enter the first governance meeting, to further evolve the roles based on tensions. Before we do that, though, there are still a few important questions that need to be answered. Who fills which role? And how is that determined? This is where another role comes in: the Lead Link.

The Lead Link role

Every circle, by default, has a number of roles that are required for the circle to function. One of these is the Facilitator role, which chairs the circle's meetings. This is the role John is temporarily filling until Neil's team is able to elect someone to take over. Neil fills the Lead Link role. So far, we haven't really gone into what that role does. Now it is time for a crash course. At first glance, the role of the Lead Link looks like a manager, but as we will see, that's not really the case. The Lead Link is appointed by the "higher" circle (or "broader", depending on how you look at it). Simply put, the Lead Link is accountable for the circle expressing its purpose. Two things come together in the name of the role: first, the Lead Link "leads" the circle and the roles of the circle (but not the people—an important difference, which we will get back to). In addition, this role makes up one half of a "double link" with the circle above it. The other half of this double link is made up by the role of the Rep Link, an abbreviation of Representative Link, which represents the circle in the circle above it. We will get back to this double linking between circles and the role of the Rep Link a little further down the line.

The Lead Link role is accountable for the circle expressing its purpose

Just like every other role, the Lead Link role has a number of specific accountabilities (see Appendix 2 for an overview). First of all, the Lead Link breaks down the overall accountabilities and authorities of the circle into specific roles. This breakdown is at the heart of what Holacracy calls "distributed authority": it goes beyond delegating into fully transferring and distributing accountability and authority into roles. This is done in the governance meeting, using a specific decision making process which we will look at in the next chapter. Whatever has not yet been distributed into a role stays on the Lead Link's plate until it becomes clear where it belongs in the circle (to which role or roles it belongs). The better the Lead Link does his or her job (role), the less involved he or she will be in the circle's operational work and the more he or she will fade into the background. This does not mean that Neil will then be out of a job; he will have merely freed his hands to fill other important roles in the circle. After all, in Holacracy, you can (and often will) fill several roles at once!

The Lead Link role carries all the accountability and authority of the circle, and continuously works to distribute and break it down into clear roles

The second accountability of the Lead Link is about assigning the roles of the circle. The roles are proposed and then evolved in the circle's governance meetings, but the question of who fills which role is answered by the Lead Link. This is one of the most important tasks of the Lead Link. The Lead Link also allocates the circle's resources, which includes allocating budget to particular roles or projects. Finally, the Lead Link translates the priorities and strategies from the higher circle and the organization as a whole into more specific priorities and strategies for the circle. In effect, the Lead Link creates the conditions within which each of the circle's roles can then autonomously make decisions and set priorities.

The Lead Link assigns roles, allocates resources, and determines the circle's overall priorities

The right people in the right roles

It is the Lead Link's accountability to assign the roles that have been created. However, the Lead Link's role does not end there: he or she is also accountable for monitoring how well circle members fill their roles, and for making changes in who fills which role, if necessary. After all, the circle performs best if people are a good fit for the roles they fill! When assigning roles, there are two paths you can follow. You can make a fresh start by assigning roles to the people that you think would be the best fit for them. That could mean making small or even big changes in the circle's division of labor. Or you can take the current reality as the starting point and assign roles based on who's currently doing that work.

By assigning the right roles to the right people, the Lead Link ensures that the circle can express its purpose

The choice between these two paths depends on what you want to accomplish and how open the circle is to making (big) changes in how things are done. In general it is recommended to use the current reality as the starting point (no drastic changes), but if you want to and are able to go faster, you could also make a fresh start. If, like Neil, you decide to take the current reality as your starting point, there is a good chance that you will have to assign some of the roles to several people, for example, because they are doing the same work, or because there is an overlap in their activities. As a start, that is not a problem. When several people fill the same role, you can optionally provide them with a "focus." An example of this would be the Sales role, with one person filling the role with a focus on Canada, another with a focus on the Western United States, and so on. In this way, it is still clear who's accountable for what, even with multiple people filling the role.

"Workable" is good enough

The Lead Link's role assignments can easily be adjusted based on tensions and new data. "Workable for now" is therefore an excellent starting point in assigning the first roles. In addition, it is wise to involve the circle in this process, especially when things change compared to the current situation. Be careful not to sweep tensions that come up during this process under the rug! The circle would not only lose important information about how things could be better, but also valuable fuel for change. How you can use these tensions as fuel is the subject of the next chapter: the governance meeting.

FOUR

THE GOVERNANCE MEETING

THE AGENDA

eil hurries through the corridor on his way to the team's first governance meeting. The first quarter is coming to an end already and he has been busy with a budget presentation all morning. Rakesh is on his case because he wants the investor to get a very positive impression. He is really counting on the North American campaign to be successful. But the team is not functioning nearly at full speed yet. Neil just assigned the roles that came out of the team's work session last week. When everybody is seated, John starts with his introduction. He explains that this meeting will be different from the team meetings they are used to.

"So, today we will not be discussing the content of the work."

Suzanne looks up. "What will we be talking about then?"

John answers, "We are going to talk about what you guys expect from each other and the way in which you collaborate. This is a discussion that is usually avoided, because it is a difficult subject and people often don't know how to start a conversation like this."

Neil nods in agreement.

"Because this is a difficult subject, we will follow a highly structured process during this meeting. For some of you, this will take some getting used to. You'll learn new things, but you'll especially learn to *unlearn* things."

Some people nod; the rest wait for what's coming.

"We'll start with a check-in. The check-in is a short round in which you each take a turn sharing what has your attention right now, so that you can let it go and be fully present."

Neil tells the group that his head is still wrapped up in the budget meeting and that he needs a moment to switch gears. When Tamara starts to respond to this, John immediately cuts her off.

"No cross-talk or discussion during the check-in." The rest of the team apparently got the message and they all keep it short. John walks over to the flip chart and invites everyone to call out tensions to build an agenda. It is quiet for a moment.

Then Will jumps in, "Usually we have a fixed agenda that we send out in advance."

"And are all the items on the agenda always relevant?"

"No, not really. Neil always makes them up ..."

Neil is quite irritated by that comment and interrupts Will, saying, "Because I expect everyone to be well prepared for the meeting. Unfortunately, I'm often the only one."

John steps in. "There is nothing wrong with preparing your own agenda items. But

if the entire agenda is defined upfront and by only one person, then those are often not the agenda items that are relevant to the whole team at the meeting."

Neil finds John's comment somewhat belittling. "Why not? I don't just put things on the agenda randomly; I think about them carefully. And I am also the one who has an overview of the whole team."

John nods. "Neil, I have no doubt that you give it a lot of careful thought. But what we are doing here is building an agenda based on tensions. Everyone here senses different things and we want all of them on the table. Then we can be sure that we are talking about real tensions and not about agenda items that seemed relevant at the time you were preparing the agenda. So ... agenda items, please."

After a bit of hesitation, the team gets going. John writes a number of agenda items on the flip chart in keywords. Neil leans back in his chair. Making up an agenda on the spot? He still has to see if that will work with this team.

4.1 ADJUSTING THE ROLES BASED ON TENSIONS

Neil and his team are now smack in the middle of their first governance meeting. It takes some getting used to, because it is very different from what they are used to. A check-in? Building the agenda on the fly? And what is the value of this governance meeting anyway? If roles are the heart of Holacracy, then the governance meeting is the heartbeat. At the governance meeting, the roles are adjusted based on tensions. This is usually done about once a month, but in the beginning it is helpful to do it more often, for example every two weeks. That will keep the momentum going; plus, a lot of tensions surface during the first few weeks. Many of these tensions were already there, but they showed up as lack of clarity, frustration, and friction. Now that we can use all that tension as fuel, a lot of energy will be freed up!

The governance meeting, where roles are adjusted based on tensions, constitutes the heartbeat of Holacracy

The purpose of the governance meeting

In most organizations, the manager determines who exactly is accountable for what. If, as a manager, you sign the Holacracy Constitution, you transfer that authority to the governance meeting process. From then on, roles and accountabilities can only be created and adjusted in the circle's governance meetings. As Lead

Link, you are still accountable for *assigning* the roles: the decision about who fills which role(s). During the governance meeting, any member of the circle can propose to add, change, or remove roles. This is done according to a highly structured process, which is enforced by the Facilitator role. Sometimes this is someone from the outside, like John, who is helping the circle get started with the new rules. Ultimately, the role will be filled by one of the members of the circle.

The structure of the governance meeting takes some getting used to. It often takes several meetings to get to know and understand the new rules. More importantly, you have to unlearn habits that have been ingrained, such as constantly interrupting each other or engaging in long discussions. It is the role of the Facilitator to enforce the structure and to cut people off where needed. If you are not used to that, it can be very confronting. And where one person's challenge will be unlearning to always immediately give his opinion, for someone else it will be to start contributing more actively. The first couple of times, the emphasis is therefore on learning and practicing the structure, and not so much on the content of the meeting. As the learning proceeds, attention to the structure will gradually fade into the background and the content of the meeting will once again be front and center. The result of a smoothly functioning governance meeting is that it is totally clear what is expected of whom and what authority you have for making autonomous decisions.

At the governance meeting, anyone can propose to add, change, or remove roles, following a rigid meeting structure

4.2 THE GOVERNANCE MEETING FORMAT

The governance meeting has a highly disciplined format, which is enforced by the Facilitator. This format consists of the following steps:

- Check-in
- Building the agenda
- Processing agenda items
- —Item 1
- —Item 2
- —Etc.
- Check-out

Check-in

The check-in marks the beginning of the meeting. Everyone takes a turn informing the circle of what has their attention, while everyone else listens. Sharing what has your attention allows you to let go of it. Instead of being distracted, you can then be fully present for the meeting. One example of a check-in would be: "I just came from a difficult meeting with a customer. I'm noticing that I'm still thinking about how to solve their problem." If others respond, or are about to go into a discussion, the Facilitator cuts them off immediately. The aim here is simply to share what's on your mind, so that the others are aware of it and you can let it go.

During the check-in, you take turns sharing what has your attention, so you can let go of it and be fully present

Building the agenda

After the check-in, the agenda is created. For many meetings, the agenda is defined well in advance. Here it is not: the agenda for the governance meeting is built on the spot. Anyone can add agenda items. Depending on the preference of the Facilitator, this can be done in random order or in a number of rounds, where everyone calls out one item until there are no more agenda items. The aim here is to create an agenda that is based on tensions. If you define the agenda upfront, it will contain items that you thought were important *at that time.* By creating an agenda on the spot, you make sure that no time and energy are wasted on matters that are no longer current or relevant. Building the agenda on the fly, however, doesn't mean you don't have to prepare! A well-prepared agenda item is often dealt with faster and more smoothly.

The agenda for the governance meeting is created on the fly, based on tensions

During agenda-building, the Facilitator captures the agenda items. Governance meetings focus on tensions about the circle's structure rather than its operations. Typical tensions on the governance meeting's agenda include a lack of clarity about what is expected from a role, what it is accountable for and what it isn't, or which role has the authority to make a decision about something. It doesn't matter whether or not others agrees with someone's tension. After all, everyone is a unique sensor for the circle and you want to fully harness everyone's capacity to sense tensions.

Moreover, at this point there's no need to explain a tension; one or two keywords are enough to add them to the agenda. They will be processed in a moment, one by one.

Sometimes it may appear more efficient to combine related agenda items and deal with them all together. In practice though, this often leads to endless discussions and watered down compromises. That is why, if several people (sensors) experience similar or related tensions, they are added to the agenda separately, so they can be processed one by one. That means that the same agenda item may appear on the agenda more than once.

The order in which agenda items will be processed is determined by the Facilitator. An open discussion about the order is rarely a good idea. Rather, you should focus on processing all the agenda items in the time available (so the order doesn't matter). Sometimes this doesn't work; especially in the beginning, agenda items may take a lot of time, because the structure is new and feels clunky. In those cases, the Facilitator is free to decide the agenda order, either with or without input from the circle. When all tensions are captured and the order has been determined, you're ready to proceed. Now each agenda item gets processed using the steps of the "integrative decision-making process" (more about this later). This process continues until either all the agenda items have been processed or you run out of time. The last five minutes of the governance meeting are set aside for the check-out.

Check-out
Whereas the check-in is intended to bring presence to the beginning of the meeting, the check-out helps close the meeting with awareness. Everyone takes a turn sharing their brief reflection on

how they experienced the meeting, without responding to each other. The check-out enables the circle to learn from the meeting. In addition, it helps you to let go of the content, so that you don't have to continue carrying it around. Finally, the habit of starting every meeting with a check-in and closing it with a check-out goes a long way towards establishing an atmosphere of openness and trust!

During the check-out, you take turns sharing your brief reflection on how you experienced the meeting, so that you can learn from it and close the meeting with awareness

As you can see, the structure of the governance meeting is pretty simple. The challenge lies not so much in this overall structure, but in how you process each individual agenda item.

THE PROPOSAL

Neil casts a doubtul look at the agenda items on the flip chart. John takes the floor again and asks Lien to explain the first agenda item.

Lien begins, "I occasionally write the company blog posts, but that isn't included in our current roles. Plus, I always send them to Tamara so that she can publish them on the website, but she often doesn't have time to do it. And I have to go to her every time I want to make a change. It just doesn't seem very efficient to me."

John asks her if she has a proposal that would solve her tension.

"I propose that we create a new role for blogs."

John writes the proposal on the flip chart: "New role: Blogmaster, accountable for ..." He looks at Lien questioningly. "What is it that you expect of this new role?"

Lien thinks for a moment and then suggests to make the Blog role accountable for publishing blogs on the website. "Oh, and updating it too, that should be part of it."

John writes: "Publishing and updating the blog"

"But ..." Tamara tries to say something, but John doesn't give her the chance.

"Just a minute, Tamara. You'll have a chance to respond in a moment, but just listen to the proposal first."

Tamara looks irritated. Neil empathizes with her because he also has to suppress his tendency to respond immediately. John explains that it is important for everyone to first understand the proposal before jumping into questions and reactions. Neil can see that the message isn't really getting through. John sees it too and explains, "Let's try it. It will become clear in the next few rounds."

Soraya cuts in, saying, "Funny, that w...," but John interrupts her before she can finish.

"As I said, I have to be very strict in my role of Facilitator. I know that you all like to give your thoughts free rein, but as you will see, this meeting is a bit more structured than what you're used to."

Soraya looks crestfallen. John's expression softens.

"Okay, let's take a quick time out. This is your first governance meeting; I know it takes some getting used to." He looks at Soraya. "What was it you wanted to say?"

"That the word 'round' reminds me of a boxing match."

"Good point! In a way it's similar to sports. You guys are the players and I am the referee. And to make sure you learn to play the game well, I have to be strict."

Will nods. "There's nothing worse than a bad referee."

John signals the end of the time-out and continues, asking, "Are there any clarifying questions about the proposal?"

"Wouldn't it be more convenient ...?" Suzanne starts. But before she can finish her sentence, John cuts her off.

"Well!" Suzanne laughs uneasily and turns to Lien, who is sitting next to her.

John explains, "Even though you are asking a question, I can tell just by the first few words that you're expressing an opinion rather than asking for clarification."

"What do you mean?"

"You don't really want to ask a question; you really want to share some thoughts on the proposal, don't you?"

"Hmm, yes, that's true."

"That's a reaction. Offering a reaction is perfectly fine, but not in the clarifying questions round. Right now, all we want is to make sure you understand the proposal. But if there are no clarifying questions, we can move on to the next round: the reaction round. I'd like to hear your reactions to the proposal. But I want to hear them one by one and without any discussion."

The opinions are divided. Some of them come up with suggestions of how it could be done differently or better. Neil notices that by going in a round, everyone has something to say, whereas in the past it was Will, Suzanne, and himself doing most of the talking. Apparently, you have to give some people time to think, or ask them for their reaction rather than waiting for them to jump in. Lien is listening and taking notes. John finally asks Lien if she wants to make any changes or clarify anything about her proposal, based on the reactions she heard.

"But remember: this is about processing *your* tension. So there's no need to do anything with these questions or reactions, unless they help you process your tension."

"So I don't have to respond to everything that was said?" Lien looks relieved.

"No, you don't, unless you want to."

Lien looks at her notes. "Someone just asked who will determine what we write about in the blog. I thought maybe we should should add something about that. The role should also be accountable for gathering subjects for the blog. And then determining which are the most interesting to elaborate on."

John writes a second accountability on the flip chart: "Collecting and prioritizing subjects for the blog"

"Like that?"

Lien nods her assent.

John continues. "Okay guys, now we're going to see if the

proposal gets adopted. We will do that in the objection round."

Neil sighs and thinks, *"Another round? When are we finally going to make a decision?"*

THE OBJECTION

eil looks at the flip chart again and reads what John wrote on it.

Role: "New role: Blogmaster, accountable for:

—Publishing and updating the blog according to the brand guidelines.

He looks at his watch, turns to John, and says, "John, the proposal is pretty clear. Is an objection round really necessary?"

John looks at Neil and signals a time-out. "Yes, it really is necessary. In fact, it's crucial. I can understand that this feels very slow to you, but there is a point to each of these steps."

"Why not skip a step if it's not needed? There is a point where you get it and can just speed up, right."

John takes a step forward. "I recognize your way of thinking, but it's a huge trap. You think, okay, we are just going to do it our own way, and before you know it, your old habits are rearing their heads and you're back where you started. The biggest mistake you can make is to take shortcuts. After all the years I've been practicing this, I still let the process do the work."

Neil is silent and sinks back in his chair.

John continues, "Okay, end of time-out! Let's continue with the objection round. An objection is a specific reason why the proposal does harm or moves us backward. For example, because it creates a new tension, or because it harms another role's ability to get its work done."

Tamara asks, "But what if I just don't think it's a good idea? Is that an objection too?"

John answers her, "No, that in itself is not a valid objection. I need to hear a specific reason."

It's so quiet in the room that Neil can suddenly hear the traffic from the street below.

He looks at the flip chart again, thinks about his roles, and wonders if there is anything in the proposal that could cause any harm ... No, he can't think of anything.

"So, objection or no objection?" One by one they each say "no objection," until John gets to Suzanne. "Suzanne? Objection or no objection?"

"I'm wondering if it wouldn't be easier to just add this to Lien's existing Copywriter role."

"Is that a reason that this proposal would cause harm, or ..."

John pauses a moment for the second part of his sentence.

"Do you actually think it is a better idea to just add this to Lien's existing role?

Suzanne nods. "Lien is already doing this anyway, so why should we create a new role for it?"

John mushes his lips together, looks at Suzanne intently: "Although I see your point, you've just told me that it's not a valid objection."

Suzanne's face turns red, as she exclaims: "Why not!"

John signals another time-out. "Because you haven't given us a reason why the proposal does harm. We're not looking for the best possible proposal here, we're looking for the simplest proposal that will solve Lien's tension while not creating any new tensions. A better idea is therefore not a valid objection. So, let's dive back in: Suzanne, objection or no objection?"

Suzanne sighs. "No objection."

John signals to go back in process, and turns to Tamara: "And do you see a reason why the proposal does harm?"

Tamara hesitates. "Actually I do."

John: "So what's the harm?"

"Well, I don't know if it is harm, but the current brand guidelines are outdated. So if this proposal would be accepted, it could harm the brand image."

John keeps asking questions, like he did with Suzanne, but this time the objection sticks. He writes it down on the flip chart.

"Neil, you were the last one. If there had not been any objections, the proposal would have been adopted. However, since there was an objection, we will now move on to the next step: the integration round. Let's see how we can integrate Tamara's objection into the proposal. This round is open, so others can help."

"You mean we're finally going to have a discussion?" Suzanne asks.

"It's not so much a discussion as helping Lien and Tamara get to a workable proposal, but yes, you're free to jump in. However, as soon as I think we may have a workable proposal, I'm going to move us back to the objection round. Tamara, do you have an idea about how to integrate your objection?"

Tamara responds, "Well, I think someone should just update the brand guidelines regularly."

Neill nods: "Yeah, that's my role, I could to that." John: "From your Brand Management role?"

Neil: "Yep."

John to Tamara: "So would you like to explicitly expect that from the Brand Manager role?"

Tamara uneasy: "Well, actually yes."

"So, what accountability would you then add to this role?

"Something like: updating the brand guidelines?"

As Tamara speaks, John writes it on the flipchart.

Neil: "Okay, so now you guys get to decide what should be added to my role?"

"Yes, that's what the governance meeting is all about."

"Hmm."

John turns to Lien. And does this still address your original tension?

"I think it does." John moves on to another objection round, based on the adapted proposal; This time there are no objections.

"Great!" John concludes. "Then the proposal has now been accepted and we have created a new role and made adjustments to another. Neil, now it's up to you, as the Lead Link, to assign the new role."

Neil breathes a sigh of relief. "I think I'm starting to get it."

4.3 INTEGRATIVE DECISION-MAKING

The first governance meeting is usually not a lot of fun. What round are we in again? Can I say something now? Usually you can't, and if you try anyway, the Facilitator will cut you off right away. Just like Neil, you might be wondering if it is really necessary to have all these rounds and strict rules. Can't we just have a normal discussion? We're all adults, aren't we?

Integrating perspectives

Making good decisions with a group of people is not easy. Often, important perspectives are ignored or dismissed because the rest of the group has a different point of view. The result is that you can lose valuable information, which has a negative impact on the quality of the decisions. At the same time, integrating *all* perspectives can take a lot of time and could lead to watered-down compromises. The integrative decision-making process used in the governance meeting allows us to hear each voice and then quickly and efficiently integrate relevant perspectives into a workable decision. A proposal is not workable if it does harm, meaning it creates one or more new tensions. These tensions form the objections against the proposal. The proposal is only accepted once these objections have been integrated in such a way that the proposal becomes workable.

Integrative decision-making gives everyone a voice and integrates the relevant perspectives into a workable decision quickly and efficiently

The governance meeting is actually nothing more than a regular meeting about the accountabilities and authorities within the circle. The roles that are established and adapted in the governance meetings define the space within which you can use your autonomy to get the work done. You could say that you are a kind of entrepreneur within your roles, with full authority to make decisions about how you energize them. In the governance meetings, the authority and the space contained in a role are constantly being adjusted, based on tensions.

Let the process do the work

The integrative decision-making steps are:
- Proposal
- Clarifying questions
- Reaction round
- Amend and clarify
- Objection round
- Integration
- (if necessary, followed by a new objection round)

When you add a tension to the agenda, that makes you the "owner" of that agenda item. You are then given the space to propose something that would solve or diminish your tension. Others can ask clarifying questions and give reactions, but the only tension you have to process is your own. You don't have to worry about anyone else's tension – if they have any, they're free to add them to the agenda so they can propose something themselves. The entire integrative decision-making process revolves around the tension owner – it's not a group discussion. In the first step, as the tension owner you are asked to present a proposal. It doesn't matter if this proposal has been fully thought through, that it's elegant or even complete. What matters is that it is a starting point; the process will do the rest.

As the "owner" of a tension, all you have to do is present a starting proposal; the integrative decision-making process will do the rest

First understand; then react

Sometimes someone has a fully developed proposal for a new role with a number of accountabilities. Other times someone may have thought about the tension but doesn't have an idea for a proposal yet. In those cases, it is sufficient to complete the following sentence: "I propose that ..." The owner of the tension is the only one that can speak at this time; the rest of the group listens to the proposal.

Once there is a proposal, you go to the next step: clarifying questions. This is where there is room for everyone to ask questions to help them understand the proposal better. Questions like "Don't you think that ..." or "Wouldn't it be better to ..." are reactions disguised as questions, not clarifying questions. If everyone gives their opinion about something that they don't fully understand yet, you will soon get bogged down in a discussion that misses the point. The Facilitator therefore immediately nips these reactions in the bud.

The owner of the agenda item is free to either answer clarifying questions, or respond with "I don't know" or "Unspecified in the proposal." There is no need for the proposer to convince the others or defend the proposal.

If there are no more clarifying questions, then it is time for the reaction round. Here, each circle members is offered a space to express a reaction to the proposal, in a round, one at a time. In the previous step, *understanding* the proposal was the main objective. Now there is room to offer your thoughts. Do you think it is a good proposal, or not? Is there something missing? What information do you want to give the owner of the proposal? The reaction round helps to get a lot of information on the table about how the proposal is being received in a short time. It is important to realize, however, that the owner is under no obligation to do anything with these reactions. It is not necessary to get buy-in or seek consensus. The only thing you're looking for is a workable proposal that will resolve or reduce the proposer's tension.

The proposal is followed, first by clarifying questions, and then by a reaction round

Before we go on to the objection round, the person who brought the proposal is given the opportunity to make any last-minute changes or to clarify something (the 'Amend and clarify' step). These are generally simple changes or brief clarifications, often resulting from something that came up during the clarifying questions or the reaction round. The Facilitator makes sure that any discussion is nipped in the bud; the only one speaking here is the owner of the proposal.

Objection or no objection?

The actual decision gets made during the objection round. Now that it is clear what the proposal entails and what everyone thinks of it, it is time to assess whether it is safe enough to try. The Facilitator asks "Do you see a specific reason why this proposal would cause harm or move us backward?"; the others answer with "Objection" or "No objection" (again: in a round, one at a time). If no one raises an objection, the proposal is accepted. If there are objections, there is one last round to integrate these objections by amending the proposal (the "Integration"), which is then followed by another objection round. An objection is defined as a specific reason why the proposal is not workable, or more specifically, why it would cause harm or move us backward. This means that the proposal, if accepted, would cause a new tension. However, not every objection is valid, so the Facilitator may ask a number of questions to test the validity of an objection.

An objection is a specific reason why the proposal is not workable; if there are no objections, the proposal is accepted

The first and foremost test question the Facilitator may ask is: "How does the proposal cause harm?" You probably have lots of ideas about how to improve the proposal, but that is not the question here! The proposal is "not workable" if it causes harm to a role, to the circle, or to the organization as a whole. "It doesn't help" is therefore not a valid objection, any more than "I have a better idea" (because it's not a reason the proposal causes actual *harm*).

The second question the Facilitator may use to test an objection is: "Is your concern created directly by this proposal?" If a tension already exists, with or without this proposal, then it's not a valid objection. If it were, you could just block every proposal simply by rehashing that same (existing) tension, and you would stop the circle from moving forward and resolving other tensions.

As a third question, the Facilitator may ask if an objection is based on data. If not, it is a fear or prediction about what might happen in the future. In most cases, knowing that you can revisit and adapt the decision as you go, is enough to cut through long discussions about what "might happen"!

Finally, the Facilitator can ask the objector which of his or her roles is limited by the proposal. What this question filters out, is people trying to think on behalf of other roles or the circe as a whole. The people filling those respective roles are in a much better place to surface those objections for their roles, if necessary.

The purpose of all these test questions is not to make it impossible to raise an objection, but rather to maintain a ruthless focus on making workable decisions that resolve real tensions, one at a time. The key questions in the objection round are: "Does it do any harm?" and "Is it safe enough to try?" If necessary, you can always propose further changes in the next governance meeting, not based on opinions and predictions, but based on actual data and real tensions!

An objection is valid only if:

1. *it is a specific reason the proposal causes harm or moves us backward;*
2. *it is created directly by adopting the proposal;*
3. *it is based on presently-known data; and*
4. *it limits one of the objector's roles.*

Integrating objections into a workable proposal

If someone has a valid objection, it is captured as specifically as possible by the Secretary. It is not necessary (or even permitted) to provide a solution at this time; the objection round is just about surfacing and capturing valid objections. If there are none, the proposal is accepted and the decision is made. If, after an objection round, there are one or more objections, then you move on to the integration step.

During integration, each objection is examined one at a time to see how it could be integrated into an amended proposal that would no longer cause those objections. No one can "block" a proposal; what you *can* do is add information that may help in integrating an objection. Integration is the only step in the integrative decision-making process where the Facilitator allows open discussion. The purpose of this is to come up with an amended proposal that would no longer cause the objections.

The basic premise is that behind every objection, there is an important perspective that needs to be integrated. Each objective is examined in order to find ways to amend the proposal into something that is safe enough to try. The objector and the proposer take center stage here, the rest of the group can help. It is not a matter or defending or convincing: the focus is on arriving at a workable decision that is safe enough to try, since we know that we can always adapt along the way if new tensions surface.

As soon as the Facilitator senses that there might be a workable proposal, he or she asks the objector(s) whether the amended proposal addresses the objection(s), and the proposer whether it still also addresses the original tension he or she set out so solve. If so, a new objection round follows for the amended proposal.

In theory, this could cycle back and forth several times, but in practice, almost all proposals are safe enough to try either immediately or after one integration cycle!

The purpose of the integration is to amend the proposal so it no longer causes the objections

Before you can master integrative decision-making, you have to unlearn your old habits and learn new ones. This generally takes at least several (frustrating) governance meetings. But once you get the hang of it, it can quickly become second nature. From then on, whenever you attend a "normal" meeting, you suddenly realize how much you have (un)learned: starting with a proposal, asking clarifying questions before reacting, separating personal opinions from role-based decision-making, asking for objections rather than endless consensus seeking. When you see with fresh eyes how ineffective conventional decision-making often is, you can wonder how most teams and organizations manage to take any decisions at all!

4.4 FACILITATOR AND SECRETARY

Every circle has a number of deafult roles that allow the circle to function. The main roles in the governance meeting are the Facilitator and the Secretary. The Facilitator chairs the meeting and the Secretary records decisions made. The most important aspect of the Facilitator's role is to enforce the meeting structure and the rules of the game. At first, it may be difficult for a Facilitator to do that well, while at the same time also contributing to the meeting from any other roles they may fill as well. That is why it can be helpful to ask someone from outside the circle, who is familiar with the rules and who has some distance from the circle's operations, to fill the role of Facilitator during the early phase of implementation.

The Facilitator role

We have seen that the Facilitator opens the meeting with a check-in and then build an agenda, based on tensions. One by one, each tension is dealt with according to the steps of integrative decision-making. If there are no objections, the proposal is accepted and then recorded by the Secretary. The governance meeting ends with a check-out. By carefully following this structure, the Facilitator helps the circle to make effective decisions about the way it is structured. The Facilitator guides the circle through the steps of the meeting, giving clear instructions about what is expected in each step. By asking specific questions (for example: "Does anyone have any clarifying questions?"or "What is your reaction to the proposal?"), a good Facilitator keeps the meeting on track, so that it feels effortless and smooth (with some practice, anyway).

The Facilitator enforces the structure and the rules of the governance meeting so that the circle can make decisions in an effective way

One of the most difficult as well as the most important tasks the Facilitator faces is to immediately cut people off as soon as they break the rules. If the Facilitator fails to do this immediately, then that opens the door for all the confusion, endless discussions, and power struggles that this structure is designed to prevent. Clearly, every Facilitator will need to find his or her own personal style of doing this, but you won't get very far as a circle with a Facilitator who can't or won't step in and cut people off when necessary (and it will be, often at first and occasionally later).

Valid output

There is a lot of wisdom in the steps and the order of the integrative decision-making process. In many cases, the Facilitator can let the process do the work, maybe jumping in now and then to ask a clarifying question, offer a helpful reaction, or even raise an objection. In fact, this is a powerful way of modeling how you can use this process to help someone process their tension. A common objection raised by the Facilitator is "Not valid governance output." You can propose anything (as long as there is a real tension underneath it), but by the time you get to the objection round, the proposal needs to have a specific format in order to be valid and accepted. You could say that integrative decision-making is like a sausage grinder: anything can go in, but only sausage comes out.

There are three types of valid outputs from governance meetings ("sausage"):

- Roles and accountabilities (creating new ones or amending existing ones)
- Policies (creating new ones or amending existing ones)
- Elections (for elected roles)

If you get to the objection round with a proposal that has a different format, then it's not a valid output (yet). After raising the "Not valid governance output" objection, it can be amended during the integration step, until it is both valid and workable. If there are no more objections during the following objection round, then the proposal is accepted.

While you can propose anything, only (new or amended) roles, policies, or elections are valid outputs of a governance meeting

The most common (valid) output of a governance meeting is a role with accountabilities. A role always consists of one or more accountabilities, all of which start with a verb (for example, "Maintaining the website"). Another governance meeting output is a policy that grants or limits authority within the circle in some way. Such a policy can be about anything; for example, it can specify a required format for requesting website updates, the rules for reimbursing travel costs, or limits on taking certain decisions, like contracting with outside parties. You could see it as a kind of ground rule that the circle agrees on for dealing with a particular subject. The third type of decision that can be made at a governance meeting is an election. In an election, the circle selects the person they think is the best fit for an elected role (for example, the Facilitator or Secretary). The process that is used for this is called the integrative election process (more about this later). Finally, these three types of governance outputs are only valid when they apply to your own circle. You cannot create roles or policies for another circle, because that would violate their autonomy. There are certainly ways of processing tensions that relate to other circles, but that's a topic we'll return to later on.

Valid objections

Any member of a circle can propose something at the governance meeting. In addition, anyone can raise one or more objections to a proposal. In order to be valid, an objection has to meet all of the following criteria:

1. It is a specific reason why the proposal causes harm or moves us backward.
2. It is a new tension that follows directly from adopting the proposal.
3. It is based on presently-known data
4. It limits one of the objector's roles.

If an objection meets all four (!) criteria, then it's a valid objection and it is recorded by the Secretary. You may be wondering why Holacracy makes it so difficult to raise objections to a proposal. There are two reasons for this. First of all, these criteria lower the threshold for decision-making. A "workable" decision is made much faster than a decision where you are trying to anticipate anything and everything. We are often not conscious of it, but for many decisions, we tend to strive for 'perfect forever', rather than 'workable for now'. With workable decisions, it becomes easier to try things out and to then make adjustments based on actual experience. Secondly, these criteria ensure that objections are based on real tensions. It is all too easy to imagine all kinds of hurdles and objections to every proposal. Some of those objections have an underlying perspective that needs to be integrated in order to make the proposal workable. But many other objections are based primarily on opinions and preferences ("how it should be") or on worries and predictions ("what might happen"). As long as there is no real data that it would create new tensions, we are better off making a workable decision. That decision can then get tested against reality, instead of trying to predict the future.

The Facilitator tests objections for their validity to maintain a ruthless focus on real tensions and workable decisions

This is one of the most important things for the Facilitator to watch out for. In every meeting, there are times when imagination gets the better of us, or fear sets in. The tendency to improve and perfect proposals, based on everything that *could* happen, gradually creeps in. Whenever that happens, it is up to the Facilitator to step in and bring the focus back to the original tension and to a workable decision. A number of Facilitator "mantras" that can help with this are:

- What is the tension?
- Is it safe enough to try?
- How can we make it workable?
- Do you have any data for that? (I.e. examples, past experiences, etc.)

If an objection turns out to be valid, it is worth recording it as specifically as possible. This makes integrating the objection into a workable proposal much easier. The objection round is finished when everyone has answered the question "Objection or no objection?" If there are no objections, the proposal is accepted; if there are objections, there is a final round: the integration. The purpose of the integration is to amend the proposal so that it no longer causes the objections, after which there is another objection round to actually test this. During integration, everyone is welcome to jump in and help, but the initiative lies with the proposer and the objector(s). Make sure you integrate the objections one at a time, instead of all of them at once, since that generally leads to consensus seeking and the tendency to aim for perfection. The Facilitator makes sure that the amended proposal still also addresses the proposer's original tension; after all, that was the whole point of the proposal!

The Secretary role

In some meetings, it is customary to record not only actions and decisions made, but also the discussion leading up to them. For governance meetings, it is sufficient to record only the final decisions. This is the accountability of the Secretary role. During the governance meeting, the Secretary keeps track of the current version of the proposal. The Facilitator can ask the Secretary to read out the current version of the proposal at any time in the process. That way you always know what you are asking clarifying questions about, offering reactions to, or raising objections to. With a good Secretary, the Facilitator has the freedom to focus entirely on the meeting process. At the end of the meeting, the Secretary updates the circle's overview of its roles and accountabilities and its policies. The Secretary is also accountable for scheduling the circle's governance and tactical meetings.

> *The Secretary records decisions, keeps an up-to-date overview of the circle's roles and policies, and schedules the circle's meetings*

THE NOMINATION

Before we continue with the election of a Facilitator and a Secretary, we will first take a break. You deserve it."

The group disperses, but Neil buttonholes Will at the coffee machine.

"How are you doing? This is something else, isn't it?"

"Yes, it definitely is. What do you think about these elections?"

"Well, what I'm thinking is that you would be an excellent Facilitator."

Will takes a sip of his coffee. "I don't know. The way John does it, I can't really see myself doing that."

"You'd certainly be a better Facilitator than me," Neil says jovially.

"Okay, guys, let's get started again," John calls out. They all go back to their seats. John stands up in front of the group and explains the election process with the ballot papers. There is some chuckling.

"Ooh, this is exciting! It reminds me of picking a prom queen!" Lien says. Her comment

elicits a few laughs.

John smiles, but adds, "Seriously now ... The prom queen is actually a really good example of how *not* to do this. The purpose of this election is not to pick the most popular person, but the person that is the best fit for the role. We will start by electing the Facilitator."

John gives a short explanation of the accountabilities of the Facilitator role. Everyone writes a name on their ballot. By now the mood has become serious. John collects everyone's ballots. He sits down and places the stack of Post-it notes in front of him. Then he picks up the top one and reads,

"Neil nominates Will."

He then asks Neil to explain his nomination.

Neil says, "Will has the most experience and he knows the most about the business out of all of us. Plus, I think he is very convincing during discussions."

Will looks uncomfortable. John picks up the next paper and reads,

"Tamara nominates Soraya."

Tamara explains, "I see her as the most structured person in our team. She may not be senior, but I think she has the qualities of a Facilitator."

After Tamara's nomination, Soraya also gets nominations from Suzanne and Will. The only paper that names Suzanne is from Lien.

John says to the group, "Having heard everyone's arguments, you can now change your nomination if you'd like. It's entirely optional, so only do it if you think someone else is a better fit for the Facilitator role. Anyone?"

Lien says she wants to change her nomination to Soraya.

"Okay, so that's clear: Soraya has the majority of the nominations," John says, looking at Soraya, who appears to be blushing slightly under everyone's attention.

"So I'd like to propose Soraya for the elected role of Facilitator."

Neil thinks it's going awfully fast. He wonders if this is it. John notices the questioning look on his face. He says, looking at Neil,

"Let's see if it is workable. We'll do the same thing we did before; we'll have an objection round."

John explains that now is the time to voice any objections to the election. He goes around the circle one by one until he gets to Neil.

"And how about you, Neil? Objection or no objection?"

Nothing from Neil ...

"Neil ...?"

"Objection."

For a moment it is perfectly quiet. Then John asks,

"Neil, can you explain your objection?"

"It's nothing personal, but I just wonder if we need someone with more experience for this role. Soraya has not been around for that long, so I doubt if she is experienced enough to keep us all in line." Neil tries not to look at Soraya as he says this.

"And is that a reason why it's not safe enough to try, knowing we can always revisit the decision by doing a new election?"

Neil's face turns red. "I don't know. ... No, no objection then, I guess."

John closes the round. No one has any further objections, including Soraya. She does have a question, however. "

Wait a minute. That means that you won't be doing it anymore, doesn't it?"

"No, definitely not," John tells her. "I will continue to facilitate during the next few weeks and I will teach you how you can best take on this role. With a bit of practice, you'll find you won't need me anymore and you can take over."

○

After Soraya's election as Facilitator, Will is elected as the circle's Secretary. No one raises objections; the team is even starting to enjoy the election process. Neil is not sure what to think of it all. He knows from experience how politics work in a company and usually he is able to play the game in such a way that he can get his candidate selected. But this time he was taken completely by surprise by the way John handled the elections. Not that he doesn't have faith in John, but what will happen after he's gone? Will he have to play things even smarter politically, or should he just trust the team?

The last part of the meeting is reserved for the check-out round. John explains that the purpose of it is to reflect on and close the meeting. He starts with Suzanne.

"To tell you the truth, this was really uncomfortable for me. I *like* having discussions. But now I'm almost afraid to say anything. I wonder if it's all too strict. It seems to me that this takes all the juice out of the meeting. Although it is probably more efficient," she ends with a note of sarcasm in her voice.

Will is next, "I have to say, I thought it was great! I like that it's so structured. In the beginning it was really slow, but when I look at the quality of the decisions we made, we did pretty well!"

When it is Tamara's turn, she has to think for a moment.

"To be honest, I find it pretty irritating when you cut people off. I am someone who tends to blurt things out ... and I'm not sure if I can change that."

Lien continues the conversation, saying, "My role became really clear to me, because of how we dealt with the proposal. The previous session where we described the initial roles was a bit too theoretical for me, but in this meeting I feel like my role has really come to life."

Soraya, after looking at Lien to see if she's finished, "For me, a real eye-opener was the difference between clarifying questions and reactions. It's so easy to jump in with your opinion. I think that's going to be a bit of a challenge."

Neil listens to the comments. He is surprised about the different reflections in the check-out. He had expected the team to show more resistance. John looks at him, as he is the last one in the check-out round.

"Honestly, I had some trouble with it. I'm used to being the chair person and now I had a completely different role. And at times it felt like it was going to go on forever; that makes me impatient and I just want to get on with it. But after hearing your check-out's and looking at the decisions we made, I'm actually pretty happy with the result, especially since it's our first time. And just like Lien, I find that this meeting really helped me to get more clarity about our roles, so that makes me feel excited to continue with this process."

4.5 INTEGRATIVE ELECTIONS

Apart from the Lead Link role, which is assigned by the higher circle, the deafult roles in Holacracy are assigned by means of elections. The purpose of these elections is to find the person that is the best fit for a role. It is not about popularity, but about the exchange of arguments: who can best fill that role and why? The integrative election process consists of the following steps:

- Description of the role by the Facilitator
- Fill out ballots
- Nomination roundNomination change
- Proposal
- Objection round
- Integration (if necessary, followed by a new objection round)

"Tamara nominates Soraya"

The Facilitator starts with a description of the role and the election term. For example, the Secretary role could be for a period of six months. Anyone can request a new election any time, but if no one does, one will be automatically triggered at the end of the election term.

When everyone understands what is expected of the elected role, each member in the circle fills out their own ballot. These can be notes or Post-its on which you write your name and the name of the person you are nominating (for example,"Tamara nominates Soraya").

The purpose of the ballot round is to gather nominations without influencing each other. The Facilitator ensures that there is no discussion and collects the nominations.

The purpose of the integrative election process is to find the best fit for a role

Next, the Facilitator reads out each ballot and asks for a brief explanation: why do you think this person is the best fit for this role? There is still no discussion at this point, but at the end of this round, everyone gets the opportunity to change their nomination, if they want to. Finally, the Facilitator will make a proposal to assign the role, based on the number of nominations. If there are several people with an equal number of nominations, the Facilitator makes a choice. Once there is a proposal on the table, the election process follows the final two steps of the 'normal' integrative decision-making process: the objection round, and if there are any valid objections, the integration. Alternatively, if there are objections, the Facilitator can choose to simply drop the proposal rather than integrate the objection, and instead propose the person with the second-most nominations. If no objections surface, the nominee is elected until another election is requested (in a governance meeting, at any time anyone feels a tension about it), or until the end of the election term.

The best fit for the role

The result of these elections is that the circle elects the people that are the best fit for the default roles of Secretary, Facilitator, and Rep Link (which, along with the Lead Link, forms the double link with the higher circle—we will see later exactly how this works).

A great side-effect of this process is that the elected person gets to hear exactly why the circle considers him or her to be the best fit for the role – something that is rarely talked about explicitly, in most teams!

An integrative election is a structured search process for the best fit for a role

All other roles in the circle are assigned by the Lead Link. Remember that like anything else in Holacracy, this is just a default and a starting point. If anyone felt a tension about how roles get assigned, they could propose a change in a governance meeting. For example, a policy stating that the Lead Link may only assign a role after stating their intent to assign in a public forum (e.g. a meeting), and giving circle members an opportunity to share their reactions to the role assignment. Or creating a new role for role assignment, separate from the Lead Link role. Whatever solves the tension!

FIVE

GETTING ROLES DONE

THE GAP

N eil has a campaign meeting with Will, Tamara, and Suzanne. So far, the preparations have been focused mainly on research and testing. Rakesh has asked Neil how the team is thinking of integrating TV and online. Will and Tamara are engaged in a heated debate and Suzanne is texting on her mobile. Neil raises his voice, and says, "Okay, everyone focus, please! Suzanne, can you give us an update about where you are?"

Suzanne looks up and visibly struggles to tear herself away from her phone. She tells them that the ad agency has come up with a strategy for the TV campaign and that their creative team is developing it now. She is expecting them to show her the initial creative images next week.

Tamara is irritated. "You already got them to develop it? My understanding from the last governance meeting was that you have the accountability to develop an integrated campaign strategy, including online."

"Oh, didn't I send it to you?"

"No, I didn't get anything."

"Oh, sorry. I thought I'd sent it. Well, anyway, as far as I can tell, the strategy was fine."

Neil sighs. "We're never going to achieve a fully integrated campaign this way." He realizes that integration is part of Suzanne's role and that it's no longer his. But he feels caught, because Rakesh looks to him for the team's progress reports.

Suzanne brushes him off. "I've done hundreds of campaigns. I certainly know how to put a campaign together!"

Neil responds wearily, "No one here questions your expertise, Suzanne. That's not what we're talking about. Last week in the governance meeting we came to a number of agreements, and you appear to be ignoring them."

"It's up to me to decide how I carry out my role! Isn't that what John said?"

Neil doesn't say anything. He doesn't know how to respond to that.

Will says, "I get where Suzanne is coming from; we've got to move forward."

Neil looks annoyed. "Yes, but we're also trying to find a way to be more aligned with each other. And what I'm seeing is that a lot of simple things are not being done or are falling through the cracks."

He turns on Will. "For example, I haven't seen that invitation that the Secretary was going to send out for the Holacracy tactical meetings."

Will blushes and looks away. "I know; I was going to send it out, but I just haven't gotten around to it yet. I've just been crazy-busy and that's on top of everything else."

"Come on, Will, how long does it take to send out a meeting invitation?"

Will is silent. Neil takes a big breath. That taste of clarity from the governance meeting seems further away than ever.

○

Neil walks back to his desk. He feels powerless. If everyone can make decisions autonomously within their roles, everyone can just do what they feel like. Won't we be worse off than before? That certainly wasn't the idea! There is still a big gap between those roles and what actually happens. After all that effort they put into de-fining them, what's the point if they're not being put into everyday practice? And Will has a point: they are all incredibly busy. Is this the right time to be experimenting?

Talking to John the next day to review the team's progress, he still feels uncomfortable about it all.

"It's not working, John."

"What do you mean?"

Neil tells him about yesterday's campaign meeting. "Nothing has changed. Isn't it just old wine in new bottles?"

The expression makes John laugh.

Neil takes offense. "It's not funny!"

"No, I know. But believe me, this is not the first time I've heard that one. And I think I understand how you feel right now."

"Something isn't working. If everyone acts autonomously with-in their roles, it's going to be chaos! They're not even managing to send out a meeting invitation. Shouldn't we try to be a little more practical? Like working on everyone's time management?"

"Neil, you'd better get used to it. Roles have real autonomy. That's always a bit scary at first, but it is true. When you fill a role, you can basically take any decision you want ..."

"What?!"

"... as long as it serves your role's accountabilities."

"So how do we make sure people actually do their job?"

"By supporting them in becoming more self-managing with-in their roles."

"Then they'll just do whatever they want."

"No, not quite. The fact that you have autonomy within your role is only part of it. With that freedom also comes responsibility."

"Responsibility. What does that even mean? Everyone has responsibility."

"That's true, but in Holacracy, that responsibility is described very specifically."

John explains that there are five basic responsibilities in fulfilling a role. Neil listens attentively.

"Yes, that really *is* specific. It reminds me of Getting Things Done. But my question remains. How is that going to help us get our act together?"

"There are some similarities with GTD, that's true, but what we're really talking about here is what specifically you can expect from each other in order to work together within your roles. If you're on a soccer team, you expect your fellow player to be able to receive the ball, pass it on, and know his position."

"Okay, I get that. But how do you make sure that really happens?"

"You hold each other accountable and you develop some key habits together. What it comes down to is that you can't actually fill a role without taking on these basic responsibilities. Because of how transparent everything becomes, there's simply no hiding from it."

Neil seems relieved. "That last part is music to my ears. Can we start with that right away?"

"The next step is to explain the basic responsibilities that come with filling a role. I call that workshop 'Getting Roles Done.' How does Friday morning sound?"

5.1 FILLING A ROLE

Neil is feeling discouraged. It sounds like a great idea, those roles and accountabilities. But if we don't put it into practice, nothing is ever going to change! At this point, the roles are still pretty much theoretical. How do you get the agreements you have made about roles to really make a difference in the day-to-day work? So that you don't end up with a "parallel universe" of theoretical roles versus actual reality!

No tension? No fuel!

There is nothing quite as discouraging as talking about how things "should" work, when you know that it won't make a difference. Instead of long, theoretical discussions, Holacracy focuses on tensions. If there are no tensions, then there's no need to have long discussions or propose changes. In fact, the Facilitator actively enforces this in Holacracy's tactical and governance meetings. In order to surface tensions though, they must be sensed first. Usually this 'sensing' happens in the course of the day-to-day work, as frustration, for example, about a needlessly complicated contract process, or an expectation you have that someone is not meeting. If you don't do anything with this, you are wasting fuel to make things better. The governance meeting bridges the gap between your everyday work and the ever-evolving agreements about how you get work done.

The tensions you come across in your everyday work are fuel for making things better—don't let them go to waste!

Freedom and responsibility

Within your role, you enjoy a lot of freedom. Governance meetings establish where the boundaries of your accountability and authority lie, but after that it is up to you how you use that freedom. However, that freedom does come with an equivalent level of responsibility. In addition to the accountabilities that are established and evolved in regular governance meetings, there are a number of basic responsibilities that every rolefiller must take on. These basic responsibilities are laid out in the Holacracy Constitution and can be summarized as follows:

1. You are a sensor for tensions
2. For each tension, you clarify what has to be done with it and where it belongs
3. You maintain a complete and up-to-date overview of current projects and actions
4. You regularly review and update this overview
5. Based on this overview, you consciously choose how you spend your time and energy

It's really pretty straightforward. You might not usually think about it in this kind of language, but you probably already do some of these things. Nevertheless, it is good to stop and think about it in a more explicit way, because this paints a clear picture of what exactly is expected from you when you take on a role. As you may have noticed, there is a clear order to these five basic responsibilities. The first one is the most fundamental: when you fill a role, you are responsible for sensing tensions for that role. In the rest of this chapter, we will see what you do next with the tensions that you sense (responsibilities 2 to 5).

Filling a role comes with a lot of freedom, but it is not without obligation: it comes with a number of basic responsibilities

A sensor for tensions

Sensing tensions is something you do all the time, whether or not you are aware of it. You continuously scan your environment and your attention automatically goes to gaps between *what is* and *what could or should be*.

Often, these gaps are experienced as problems or threats. You either resist them or try to convince others to do something about them. Uncomfortable tensions are swept under the rug or simply ignored. Or you can simply blow off steam at the coffee machine or at home, over dinner. The negative charge we often experience with tensions is caused by all kinds of judgments, beliefs, and fears. No matter how often we say that tension is fuel, this negative charge doesn't just disappear overnight. Learning to work with tensions is a slow process of building trust. If you can let go of the belief that you must always and immediately have the answer or the solution, that will create space for you to observe without judgment. That's when you really become a sensor for your roles and for the organization. The meetings and the Holacracy Constitution will then provide you with the leverage to truly begin to use those tensions as fuel for continuous improvement.

The more you can let go of the belief that you must have a solution for every tension, the better you can be a sensor for your roles and the organization

5.2 PROCESSING TENSIONS

From your role, you are constantly scanning your environment for gaps between how things are and how they could be. So you are a sensor for tensions. But then what? What are you supposed to do with those tensions? This is where the other four basic responsibilities come into play. You start by creating clarity: should you do anything with this specific tension? And if so, what? You add the actions and projects that result from that clarity to your overview of projects and actions, so it stays complete and up to date. Finally, you make conscious choices in the moment about what you are going to do, based on that complete overview. People who have experience with GTD will recognize the five steps for individual productivity, which David Allen distinguishes: capturing, clarifying, organizing, reviewing, and doing. Capturing, in Holacracy, means that you are a sensor for your roles, for the circle, and for the organization and that you systematically capture the tensions you sense. Let's see what the follow-up steps look like from the perspective of the circle and the roles.

"Not my role!"
Not every tension you pick up can or should be resolved by your role. The second basic responsibility that comes with filling a role is to clarify what to do with a tension and where it belongs. There are a number of questions that can help you process a tension:
- Does your role care about this tension?
- Does another role within your circle care?

- Does your circle care?
- Does the organization care?
- Do you care personally?

The questions are in order: you start at the top and end at the bottom. If the answer to all the questions is "no," you can simply let go of the tension. Apparently, this particular tension you sensed does not provide any relevant information either for the organization or for you. In most cases, you will probably answer "yes" to at least one of the questions. If you think a tension is relevant for the organization, a specific circle, or another role, then something should be done about it, but not by you. It may concern a request you received for something that another role or circle is accountable for. Or maybe you read something in the newspaper that gets you thinking about what the organization could or should do.

In Holacracy, everyone is an entrepreneur within his or her roles. If a tension touches on one of the accountabilities of a role you fill, then it is up to you to decide what to do with it. This applies to other roles too, of course, so whenever a tension belongs elsewhere, all you have to do is pass it on to the right circle or role. As a comparison: say you notice that your neighbor's car has a flat tire (a tension). Are you going to get to work replacing his tire? If you want to be a helpful neighbor, you simply let your neighbor know that he has a flat tire. Or maybe you don't do anything and just trust that your neighbor will notice it and take care of it himself. What it boils down to is that it is not *your* tension. And so it is not your job to resolve it.

If it is not part of your role to resolve a tension, just pass it on to the right role or circle, or let go of it

In many organizations, it is a sign of engagement and commitment to concern yourself with things that you are not (directly) accountable for. No matter how well-intentioned, you're really perpetuating the problem, which is that it's currently not (sufficiently) clear who is accountable and what is expected from whom. By defining clear and explicit roles and accountabilities, you know exactly who you can count on for what. If it is not clear who is accountable for something, resist the temptation to jump in and "rescue" the organization by solving it yourself. In Holacracy, this is called "individual action": action outside of your (current) roles and accountabilities. You could say you're doing it in a personal capacity. There is absolutely nothing wrong with taking individual action, but if it keeps happening, it means you need to create more organizational clarity. You can do this simply by bringing it to the next governance meeting, so that you can create clarity about where that particular accountability belongs. So, individual action is fine, but make sure it does not turn into a pattern. In this way, the organization can continuously learn from new tensions!

If you make a habit of "rescuing" the organization, you deprive it of the opportunity to learn from the tension and increase organizational clarity

Next-actions and projects

If a tension touches on one of the accountabilities of a role you fill, it is up to you to deal with it. Sensing tensions happens naturally; you register tensions all the time, consciously or not. Unfortunately, the same is not true for processing and clarifying those tensions: that requires conscious thought. What is the tension?

What is needed? What is the next step? And if that doesn't solve the tension, what will? What does the desired outcome look like? This kind of disciplined thinking results in a list of next-actions and a list of projects (desired outcomes). Holacracy borrows the definition of projects and next-actions from Getting Things Done. A next-action refers to a physical, visible activity. This is not about a list of possible, future actions, but about the *first, next* action needed to move forward. Examples of next-actions are:

- Call Denis regarding the campaign's progress
- Download reimbursement form
- Read research report
- Invite Tamara for meeting about customer mail-out
- Create first draft of Q3 budget

Thinking in terms of next-actions helps you process a vague tension into a very specific follow-up step. The objective is to formulate the action in such a way that you no longer have to think about it and therefore you can carry it out immediately. If the next-action is not clear enough (for example, "reimbursements"), you will have to stop and think again about what is needed and what the next-action is, when you want to get it done. Chances are that this will become one of those things that you feel resistance to (because it is not clear) and that you keep putting off (until it becomes urgent enough to stop and think about).

A next-action is the physical next step you take to resolve or diminish a tension

The downside of thinking only in terms of next-actions is that you pay less attention to the bigger picture and to what needs to be achieved *after* taking that next-action. If something is not finished after taking the next-action, it makes sense to also clarify what the desired outcome should be. You do this by defining a "project". In Getting Things Done as well as in Holacracy, a project is defined as a desired outcome that requires more than one action. Projects, according to this definition, can refer to relatively small outcomes, instead of the complex, longer-term outcomes that we usually think of as projects. A project is formulated as a desired outcome, as if it were already true. The question you answer is:

"What will it look like when it's done?"

A few examples of projects are:

- Campaign plan written
- Contract X signed
- Blog post about product Y published
- Budget Q3 approved
- Holacracy implemented

A project is a desired outcome that takes more than one action to achieve

The decision about when something is "done" is subjective, of course. For each of these examples, you could ask if the project will truly be done once you achieve this outcome. In many cases, there is a still larger goal or outcome, so that you are actually not quite done yet, or maybe never will be. The latter takes us to the domain of roles and accountabilities, which, as you know, refer to ongoing or recurring activities.

In this way, you can distinguish between three levels of thinking about and defining your work:

1. Roles and accountabilities
2. Projects (defined as desired outcomes)
3. Next-actions

When you have clarity on all three levels, then you know exactly what can be expected of you (your roles and accountabilities). These ongoing activities generate more specific desired outcomes, which you add to your project list. Finally, for every project you define a next-action, which you add to your action list. These two lists (projects and next-actions) form the basis of the system you use to keep track of your work.

5.3 COMPLETE AND CURRENT OVERVIEW

Capturing and then processing tensions are two of the basic responsibilities of filling a role. The third one is organizing the outputs of this in a complete and current system that contains all of your projects and next-actions.

In addition to a projects list and a next-actions list, such a trusted system could include other lists, for example:

- "Waiting for" list (things you are waiting for from something or someone)
- "Someday/maybe" list (things you are not committing to doing right now, but which you may want to take on in the future)
- Agenda items for the governance meeting (specific tensions about expectations, roles, and policies)
- Agenda items for the tactical meeting (specific tensions about operational issues)

Would you like to find out more about how you can set up a trusted system? Just do a search for "Getting Things Done" on the internet, or better yet, read the book with the same name by David Allen. In the back of this book, you will find a short summary of the method (Appendix 1).

Your list of projects and your list of next-actions form the heart of the system you use to keep track of your roles' work

The key point here is not which lists to use, but to break the habit of keeping everything in your head. There are two reasons why this is absolutely critical. The most important one is David Allen's argument: your head is not built to do this! The capacity of your working memory to remember things is quite limited. On average, you can't actually store more than seven things at a time in your working memory. As soon as something new is added, something else is lost (at least until it gets triggered again, and crowding out yet another issue in turn).

So, you need an "external memory," and that is exactly what your overview of current projects and next-actions is. On top of that, by relieving your working memory, you are freeing up space for issues that your brain is much better at, such as sensing tensions, recognizing patterns, and coming up with new ideas. And it just so happens that these are exactly the kinds of things you *cannot* outsource to an external memory!

Break the habit of keeping current projects and actions in your head: your brain is not built for it, and they take up precious attention that could be better used for other, more valuable things

The second reason not to keep your overview in your head (or rather, to continue to make the rather futile attempt) is a more practical one. When you've got everything in your head, it is much more difficult to make conscious and transparent choices about what's most important now, considering everything that's on your plate. It should be pretty obvious why you want to make conscious choices, rather than going with the 'latest and loudest,' as David Allen calls it. But why should these choices also be transparent? If you work alone, maybe they don't. But most of us need to work with others in service of a larger purpose. In those cases, transparency is a fundamental part of being able to coordinate and do the work.

A complete and current overview of your projects and next-actions helps you make conscious and transparent choices

5.4 WEEKLY REVIEW

No matter how complete and current your overview is, if you don't maintain it, it will be outdated in no time. Filling a role means that you regularly update your overview of that role's current projects and next-actions. This is where the 'weekly review' comes into play. The weekly review is the fourth of the five basic responsibilities of filling a role and, according to David Allen, it is by far the most important ingredient for individual productivity. If you fail to 'install' this habit, not only will your own productivity suffer, but you will also likely become the bottleneck for your team's overall productivity.

A weekly meeting with yourself
The weekly review is, in effect, a "meeting with yourself," where once a week you take the time to empty your head and bring your external memory up to date. Just like the governance meeting, a meeting with yourself has a number of steps:
- Capturing tensions and open loopsProcessing and organizing them
- Reviewing your listsConsciously choosing your priorities for the week

By doing the weekly review, you empty your head and update your trusted system, so that it is complete and current again

The review begins with capturing everything you still have to "do something about," whether they are notes, emails, or thoughts. Don't worry about what to do with them and don't think about them—all you are doing at this stage is collecting them. Think of this process as building an agenda for the meeting with yourself. One or two keywords per item should generally be enough.

When capturing tensions and open loops, it can be helpful to run through this 'trigger list' and consider if they trigger anything you need to do something about:

- Notes, letters, voicemails, documents, downloads, etc.
- Your unread (or unprocessed) emails from the past week
- Last week's calendarYour upcoming weeks' calendar
- Your "waiting for" list
- Your "someday/maybe" list
- Your current roles and accountabilities (at least once a month)
- Your head (everything that is still floating around in there that you have to do something about)

By now you should have managed to collect a good number of tensions and open loops. Now go over them one by one and clarify each item. The key to success is to finish your thinking process for each of these issues, every time, one at a time. What exactly do you need to do with that note? And this email? Does any of your roles care? If so, formulate the next-action and (if that does not finish it) the desired outcome (project). If your roles don't care, hand it over to a role or circle that does, or let it go. If it takes less than two minutes to solve something or get it done, do it immediately. After all, it takes longer to add the action to your system and review it later, then to quickly take care of it now. David Allen calls this the '2 minute rule'. You are done when you have clarified and organized each item in your system by adding it to the right list (for example, next-actions, projects, someday/maybe, tactical meeting, governance meeting, etc.).

Start your weekly review by systematically collecting tensions and open loops and then clarifying them into next-actions and projects one at a time

The next step is maintenance of your system. Go over the lists to make sure they are complete and current:

- Next-actions (Are they clear? Do they refer to the *first* next step you need to take to move forward?)
- Projects (Is the desired outcome clear? Is it still accurate? Is there at least one next-action on your action list for each project?)
- Roles and accountabilities (Do they still make sense? Do you want to take up any new projects? Do you have any agenda items for the governance meeting?)
- Waiting for (Are they still current? Do you need to follow up on anything?)
- Someday/maybe (Is there something on there that you might want to activate? Is there anything you want to take off the list?)

Now that your overview is complete and current again, you can make conscious choices about what you want to work on this week. How will you distribute your energy and attention among your many roles, projects, and actions? What will you do now and what can be delayed until later? Go over your project list and select the projects you choose to work on this week. Be realistic when you prioritize, and consciously choose not only what you *will* do, but also what you will *not* do this week.

> *Looking at your updated overview, now make conscious choices about what you want to work on this week*

Finished reviewing your system and setting priorities? Then the rest of the week all you have to do is look at the selection of prioritized projects and actions. Selecting what you *will* do provides focus; selecting what you will *not (yet)* do provides peace of mind!

From reactive to proactive

It is important to maintain the connection between your role(s) and accountabilities and the day-to-day reality of projects and next-actions. Religiously doing the weekly review is one of the keystone habits in achieving this conscious and pro-active work mode, rather than reacting to the latest and loudest. Whereas next-actions and projects are always finished at some point, the accountabilities that come with your roles describe the ongoing activities that you're expected to maintain. If you forget to review these even for a few weeks, holes will begin to show up in your system. To prevent this, make sure you review your roles and accountabilities at least once or twice a month as part of your weekly review. Reviewing overall progress and prioritizing projects is mostly needed on a weekly basis, to make sure projects don't stall and you have clear next-actions for each of them.

By doing the weekly review, you maintain the connection between your roles and your day-to-day work, and you enable yourself to make conscious, proactive choices

THE PROMISE

During the first part of the Getting Roles Done workshop, John talked about the five basic accountabilities and how to put them into practice. Neil is happy to see that it makes sense to everyone. Soraya had commented that they already work like this on days when everything is going well. During the last portion of the workshop, John talks about the fifth accountability: how do you consciously choose and prioritize what to work on?

"This accountability basically means that you make a conscious decision at every moment. You know your next-action list is complete, so now you can decide what your priorities are. Does anyone have their to-do list handy?"

Neil looks around, but no one says anything, so he offers, "We have last team meeting's action list. Will that do?"

"Yes, that's fine." John picks up the list and reads, "What is the first action point?"

Tamara answers, "That one is mine. I was going to do a mail-out to the customer base."

"So it can get crossed off?"

"No, I didn't do it yet, because ..."

John interrupts her.

"There is no need to explain why it didn't get done. I'm just curious why you put today's date on it."

"Um ... because last week I assumed that I'd be able to do it."

"And then you knew for sure?"

"No."

"Why did you provide a date if you weren't sure?

Tamara's face turns red. Neil feels that John is going a little too far and interrupts him.

"John, listen, I asked Tamara for a deadline last week, simply because on our action list we never leave things open. Otherwise, anyone can say anything and then it's not really a commitment."

"Okay, I get that. You want clarity. But do you have that now? Is it clear when this will be done?"

Tamara says, "No, it isn't and I want to say something about this because I feel that I'm being put on the spot here. The reason I gave that date was because I felt I had to live up to everyone's expectation that it would be done by then. But to be honest, I had so many other things to do this week that, in retrospect, I shouldn't have made that promise."

John acknowledges her, saying, "Thanks, Tamara." He turns to the group. "Does that happen often?"

"We often push most of the action points forward in time because we're all so busy," Suzanne says.

"Right. And so you hope that if you put a deadline on it, then it will get done."

Suzanne nods. "Exactly."

"I understand you can't leave this open-ended, but by demanding a 'by when' from each other on every action point, you're really just fooling each other."

Will speaks up. "Sorry, John, but I disagree with you. By putting a date on it, you make it more real."

"I will get back to that in a minute, Will. Because there is a catch here. In order to live up to the third basic accountability, you have to be able to show a complete overview of your work at any time. If a team member needs to know what you're working on, you have to able to give him an overview of your current projects."

Neil asks, "But that doesn't mean anything if there is no specific planning, does it?"

"No, I don't agree with you. A 'by when' does not necessarily make it more clear. It is much more important to be able to indicate which project has priority over other projects. Let's do another exercise: I want you to write down the desired outcomes of your current projects on Post-its and then arrange them in order of importance from the top to the bottom."

John passes out Post-its. Everyone starts writing feverishly.

After a few minutes, John looks around the room and asks,

"Is everyone done?" He walks over to Tamara. "Tamara, if you were to look at your projects this way, would you have committed to that deadline as readily?"

Tamara straightens. "I don't think so."

"Why not?" John wants to know.

"I gave that date without having the overview. Now that I look at it, I realize that there was no way I would have been able to get to it, because there is another, much more important project on my plate."

Will says, "But how do you stay on top of it all without clear deadlines?"

"What do you mean by 'on top'?"

"That you know it will get done."

John turns back to the group. "You can give each other transparency on the relative priority of your projects. Then you'll have a much more reliable overview than picking a random date. You'll be in a much better place to give a realistic estimate of when something will likely get done, given your current priorities."

Lien interjects, with a slight tone of disbelief, "But, John, how do you do that on a daily basis? For example, I like to write down at the beginning of the day what I'm going to do and then cross off the items I've done. That's a lot easier."

John smiles. "Yes, it does sound easier. But, be honest now—do you always finish your list at the end of every day?"

Lien sighs. "No, actually I almost never do. I always seem to bite off more than I can chew."

John takes a step back and asks, "Sound familiar, anyone?"

Everyone nods.

"And do you realize that you are in effect doing the same thing as Tamara? Giving a date and then having to admit she can't do it by then? What I'm trying to say is that even on the level of your everyday tasks, you should set priorities rather than making a definite plan."

"But how do you do that?" Soraya asks.

John looks at her. "Before you do anything, you look at your list, or your lists, preferably grouped by into the type of activity or context you're working in, and based on that, you determine what is the most important thing for you to start working on."

"But how do I know what is the most important?" Will asks.

"If I gave you fifteen minutes, and a list of ten customers you could call, you would probably know exactly which ones you'd be calling during that time period. If you have a reliable overview of everything that you could be doing, you can use your intuition to pick the most important thing to work on now."

Neil understands what John is saying. But something is still missing.

O

Neil walks down the corridor to his office. He sits down at his desk and looks over the action list from the meeting again. Yes, those dates—it's true; they do push them forward most of the time. But he likes to have them around when Rakesh or someone else asks about the progress of a project. If the team were to start working in John's way, he would find himself in a difficult position. After all, many of the projects they work on have strict deadlines. Isn't this a step backward instead of forward? He walks back over to the boardroom and sees that John is still there, working on his laptop. When Neil comes in, John looks up.

"What's up, Neil?"

"Well, I was just thinking some more, John. And the lack of planning is kind of bothering me."

"What do you mean?"

"Well, what you say makes sense. We hardly ever come through on our action deadlines. But the reality is simply that the rest of this company wants me and my team to give them a solid deadline. There is just no way for me to get around that."

John looks at Neil curiously. "'Reality'—that's an interesting thing."

Neil frowns. "You're being a bit philosophical."

"Maybe, but what I'm talking about right now is not: Are you really grounded in reality when you give someone a so-called solid deadline that is based on wishful thinking? Or are you just pleasing them by telling them what you think they want to hear?"

Neil feels like he is being driven into a corner. "But you can't deny that deadlines work! They motivate people. If we hadn't had such a strict deadline for the North-American campaign, we probably would have never started with Holacracy."

John says, resolutely, "Sure, deadlines can create a sense of urgency. But what I'm trying to say is that using deadlines as a way of keeping control and managing your day-to day work will always get you into trouble."

"It's better than nothing, isn't it?"

John concedes, "It sure is. But I'm not advocating going back to nothing. What I'm suggesting is using realtime projections rather than blind promises."

"What's the difference?"

"If I tell you off the top of my head that I'll be in Portland in three hours, that's a promise. But if I'm driving through rush-hour traffic, my navigation system will give me a realtime overview of all the information about different routes and where the blockages are. Now I can give you a realistic projection of when I will be in Portland. because I have access to much more information. The question is: how do you and your team want to steer? Based on promises, or based on realtime information?"

"Based on information, of course."

"Okay, then that's what we'll start doing in the next tactical meeting. I will need an overview of all the key metrics that are important to the team. As Lead Link, you are accountable for defining and assigning the circle's metrics. Can you prepare those for the next tactical meeting?"

"All right, I will."

5.5 PLANNING VS. PRIORITIZING

Planning—it is something you do every day to one degree or another. But is it really as effective as we think it is? And are there alternatives? Tamara commits to a deadline, even though she already knows she's probably not going to be able to make it. Neil's planning appears to give him some peace of mind. But the problem with planning is that we are not very good at estimating how long something will take. On average, we are wrong about fifty percent of the time, and that is being optimistic. In addition, planning is by definition based on predictions of the future. The idea that reality will unfold based on our plans is an illusion, of course. But it is an illusion that gives you a comfortable sense of certainty and control! It becomes even more dangerous if you put a lot of energy into maintaining this illusion of control. Then you're confusing your plan with reality, and reality has a way of winning that battle.

A more dynamic way to steer and make choices about your work is to prioritize. When you prioritize, you do not make a prediction about how long something will take or when exactly you will do it. Instead, you use your trusted overview of everything you could be working on. When you have a complete overview, you can make conscious choices instead of blindly promising when something will be done. You can also offer others transparency about the choices you make and the priorities you set. If you want to give more priority to something, that automatically means that something else will not get done or will get done later. By being transparent about these choices, you invite others to take responsibility for the requests they make. If on top of that, you offer transparency proactively, in short cycles (such as regular team meetings), then others will be able to see your progress as you go, and make adjustments when needed. Doing this actually gives you *more* control than a static, upfront plan with deadlines that you hope you'll be able to meet. And when you don't meet them, you usually won't know until the last minute or even afterwards. Prioritizing provides less certainty, but it is a lot more realistic and flexible than planning!

Prioritizing based on a complete and transparent overview gives you a lot more actual control than planning based on predictions and deadlines

And if you need to (for example, because of external circumstances or a deadline for a client), you can always go back to planning and deadlines for that. But even then, you will have a lot more information about what's on your plate and how a promise impacts everything else you have going on!

5.6 ROLE-BASED COLLABORATION

Sensing tensions, maintaining an overview of your projects and actions, making explicit choices about how to spend your time and attention, doing your weekly review... There's a lot that is expected from you when you take on a role. And that's just filling your *own* roles!

What can you expect from each other?

No role can achieve the circle's purpose alone. Although most work gets done *within* roles, there are often many connections and interdependencies *between* roles, too. Without collaboration, a circle cannot function. What exactly can you expect from each other? And what do you do when someone does not meet those expectations? These are essential questions! Usually, they have as many answers as there are people on the team. Everyone has their own perception, which gets surfaced only when something goes wrong (and sometimes not even then). Ask people to write down what they think is expected from them and what they expect from others on the team. You will be surprised at how different their expectations are! This is why we have regular governance meetings in Holacracy. During the governance meeting, you define what can be expected from each role. This is not a one-time, ad-hoc discussion; it's a regular one, so that expectations can be constantly adjusted on the basis of real tensions and changing circumstances.

It is important to align expectations regularly and explicitly

In addition to the specific accountabilities that come with a role, we often have more general expectations from each other in working together. How do you hold a colleague accountable when she doesn't energize one of her role's accountabilities? And what can we request from one another? Let's look at a few examples:

- Which projects and actions do you have in your Sales role?
- How have you prioritized your projects and actions?
- When do you estimate this project or action will be finished?
- What is your next-action on this specific accountability or on that project?
- Can you take on this project or that action?

Dealing with requests

The expectations as established in the governance meeting are central to making requests among circle members. The key question that you ask yourself when someone makes a request is "Does my role care?" If the answer is "no," then make that explicit: "That's not my role." That doesn't necessarily mean that you personally don't care or that you won't do it; even though it's not your role, you may still want to pick it up (as 'individual action'). But whether you pick it up or not, make sure you bring it to the next governance meeting, so that a conscious decision can be made about it. Then it will be clear the next time around!

As you can see, things get very transparent with Holacracy. When you take on a role, other circle members have the right to make requests about the projects and actions you take on, about how you prioritize them, and about when you estimate any one of them will get done.

In Holacracy, circle members have the right to ask for transparency on how you choose to energize your role

When it comes to making requests and giving transparency, keep two things in mind. First, you don't want to create fuzziness and confusion about what can and cannot be expected from a role. That is what the governance meeting is for. The second important point is that you reliably keep track of all projects and actions that you take on in your roles. That is why the weekly review is such a keystone habit. If you are clear on your priorities, it's pretty easy to provide a realistic estimate of when something will be finished. An estimate is not a promise, by the way; it is based purely on what you know now and what you can foresee. If tomorrow, someone wants to know if anything has changed, you can always give a new estimate. All in all, a lot is expected of you when you take on a role, but on the other hand, you can ask circle members to provide you with that same level of clarity and transparency!

SIX

THE TACTICAL MEETING

PROGRESS

Neil is surprised when he walks into the boardroom. The whiteboard on the wall has been divided into a grid of rows and columns.

"How do you like my artwork? Looks impressive, doesn't it?" John says while he continues writing on the board.

"To each his own," Neil says, smirking. "Is this for our tactical meeting?"

"Yes, it is. This is the first version of our project board."

Five minutes later, all the team members have arrived. John has arranged the room so that everyone can see the board. He explains that the purpose of the tactical meeting, which they are now going to experience for the first time, is to sync up operationally, so that everyone can move forward with their work.

"Just like in the governance meeting, we'll be doing this in a highly structured way. But this time we won't start with building the agenda. Instead we will do a couple of quick update rounds first."

Neil wants to know, "Won't we run out of time, if we only have one hour?"

"The update rounds help everyone get up to date and provide input for the agenda." John points at the project board and explains what is on it and how they will use it. "But, first things first, let's start with a check-in."

After a few check-ins, it is Neil's turn. "I'm very curious about this meeting. To tell you the truth, after the Getting Roles Done workshop, I wonder what the added value of the tactical meeting is."

When they get to the checklist review round, Neil is happy to be able to share that he did his weekly review. He is surprised to hear that several other people also answer "yes" to this checklist item. Not everyone quite yet, but definitely progress! During the next round, John asks several roles to report on the circle's metrics. Neil is curious to see how the others do, since usually he is the only one presenting any numbers. To his surprise, the team turns out to be well-prepared. Will especially seems to enjoy presenting his role's metrics, which incidentally gives Neil some valuable input for the status update he'll be presenting next week. Next, John asks everyone to write down their current projects on Post-its and stick them on the project board. A few minutes later, the board is covered with Post-its.

"Great, then we're ready for the project round now. We are not going to discuss each project in detail; just give us a short update or say 'no change' if there is nothing to report."

When it is Suzanne's turn, she says, "no change" about each of her projects. John can see that Tamara wants to say something, but he jumps in.

"If you guys have something to say, please hold it until we build the agenda. Then we'll collect everything at once."

Tamara writes something down on her notepad. About fifteen minutes later, John indicates it's time to build the agenda. The team looks a bit ill at ease.

"Are we supposed to just make it up on the spot?" Lien asks.

"No, don't make anything up! Just see if you feel any tension around anything. It could be an operational issue that's been on your mind, or maybe the rounds we just went through triggered something for you."

John gives them a few minutes and then asks, "Okay, agenda items, anyone? Just one or two keywords per item, please. It's just a label, we'll dive into them later."

Pretty soon, there's a list of about a dozen agenda items on the flip chart.

"And we're going to get through all of these in the time remaining?" Will asks, frowning.

"Yes, we are" John says, with a reassuring smile.

That would be amazing, Neil thinks to himself.

THE NEXT-ACTION

The first agenda item is Tamara's. The flip chart says "online campaign." John asks her, "Can you tell us more about your tension?"

Tamara explains that she doesn't feel good about how the online part of the campaign is developing. "I had a look at what Suzanne's ad agency has been doing so far, and I have a few questions about it. It includes figures that are just not realistic. I am wondering if they have the expertise that we need for this campaign."

Suzanne wants to react, but John interrupts her.

"Just a minute, you can respond in a moment. First I want to hear from Tamara what she needs here."

Tamara looks at Suzanne and then at John. "Good question. I think I want to make sure that the online part of our campaign is going to be successful."

"And which role are you asking?"

"Well, in particular to Suzanne."

"In what role?"

"In her Campaign role."

Suzanne asks, "What is it that you think they're missing?"

Tamara responds, "SEA is estimated much too low and SEO much too high. SEA is a tricky thing. It's kind of like an auction; if you set it up wrong, you can lose a lot of money."

Neil jumps in. "If that's true, that is a problem. We really can't go over budget."

Will begins, "But how can ...?"

John intervenes. "Sorry guys, but I need to interrupt here. A short discussion to clarify the issue is absolutely fine, but we're not trying to solve the problem here and now. Rather, the question we need to answer is: what is the next-action?"

All is quiet for a moment. Then Tamara says, "I propose that we engage a specialized agency to deal with our campaign's SEA and SEO."

Suzanne leans forward, about to jump in, but John beats her to it. "And whose accountability is that?"

Suzanne responds, "Isn't that my accountability? I am the one directing agencies."

Neil adds, "It is your accountability to direct ad agencies. But what Tamara is talking about is not an ad agency."

Suzanne mutters under her breath.

John: "So, do I gather that it's not entirely clear who is accountable for this?"

"Right."

"Then I propose as a next-action that Tamara prepares a proposal about this for the next governance meeting."

Tamara, surprised about the unexpected turn, says, "But, John, does that mean I have to wait until the next governance meeting to move forward with engaging an online agency?"

"Absolutely not, that would really slow you down. You can use your autonomy and do what is needed until then. In Holacracy, this is called an 'individual action'."

"What is that?" Tamara asks.

"An individual action is an action you take outside of your current roles. You can always do this, provided that you also bring it to the next governance meeting, so that you can solve the issue on a more ongoing basis, rather than continue to take individual action."

"Makes sense."

John turns to the team again: "So, to wrap up this agenda item, what is the next-action for engaging an online agency?"

Will looks at Neil and says, "Didn't you have an agency that you worked with in the past?"

"Yes, I was very happy with them. Tamara, I will give you their phone number."

"Okay," Tamara says. "I've got it. Will, could you write down a next-action for me: 'Phone online agency'."

Will makes a note and then looks back up, "So what is the desired outcome? 'Online agency found?'"

Tamara answers, "Okay, how about, 'Online agency briefed.'"

Will nods approvingly and writes it down.

THE RHYTHM

After the first agenda item, processing the rest of the items goes fast. After one hour, they end the meeting with a check-out. When all the team members have filed out, Neil is left with John.

Neil looks at his watch. "That was fast! I think we must have set a speed record."

John smiles, "Yes, it was. A tactical meetings can be very fast. But speed is not the goal."

"So what is the goal?"

"The goal is to process all the agenda items in the allotted time, regardless of how many there are. We had quite a few today, so I decided to speed it up."

Neil pours a glass of water. "I still have to get used to all this. I would have liked to have more of a discussion about some of the topics. It feels a little open-ended."

John looks at him. "You would have liked to have more space for discussion?"

Neil takes a sip. "Yes, I'm afraid we won't get around to it if we don't do it here, with everyone around the table."

"I can relate. But there are two problems: First of all, it is no longer up to you, but up to the relevant roles to make decisions and do the work. And secondly, if you try to do everything in one meeting, you end up doing none of it well."

John continues, "

What you're looking for, is for everyone to be involved in

every decision. But that's an extremely inefficient way of working together."

Neil sighs. "Yes, you've got a point. But I just like to jump in and get things done."

"Of course; there is nothing more satisfying than making real progress and ticking things off the list. But that happens outside of meetings, by people driving their roles and making decisions autonomously. The meetings are just there to sync up and remove obstacles, so that everyone can go back to the work of their roles."

Neil's not sure. "Hmm ... so how do I know if people are making the right decisions, and if we're on track?"

"Did the old meetings give you that type of control?"

"Well, a little bit. But there was never time enough to cover it all, so I would have to follow up constantly, in between meetings."

John asks Neil, "Takes a lot of time, doesn't it?"

John replies, "Yes, it does. Sometimes it feels like it's all I do."

"So, you're constantly checking in with people, a few minutes here, a few minutes there, squeeze in a quick email ..."

"Right ... how do you know that?"

John sighs. "Working in this ad hoc way is a huge productivity killer. You're continuously interrupting each other. When you establish a reliable rhythm of weekly tactical meetings, you will end up needing much less alignment in between. And that will free up a lot of time, for everyone."

Neil, surprised, says, "That does sound good! But I'm wondering about one more thing. You say the tactical meeting generally happens once a week. But you can't always afford to wait until the next meeting, can you?"

"That's right, sometimes you can't," says John. "Remember that you can still talk to each other and find alignment outside of Holacracy's meetings. But if this is a big issue for you, you could consider adding another, optional meeting. It's called the 'daily stand-up'. Why don't we try it tomorrow?"

Neil puts his hand up. "Hold on. Let me get this straight: you're asking me to simply trust that things will ultimately get done simply because of this meeting rhythm?"

"Exactly. These regular meetings will give everyone on the team complete transparency. You will know exactly what is going on, and because of the shortened cycle, you get to constantly steer and adapt based on real tensions."

"Okay, let's do it!"

"That's the spirit," John says.

6.1 ALIGNING THE CIRCLE'S WORK

Clarity about roles is important, but it is not a goal in and of itself. Ultimately, the circle's work is the focus. For this reason, and next to the governance meeting, Holacracy also has operational meetings. The most important type of operational meeting is the tactical meeting, but you can also consider having short daily meetings (the stand-up—more about this later). To be clear, the tactical meeting can never completely replace other ways of getting aligned about the day-to-day work. At the same time, we're all familiar with the constant interruptions of "short" meetings and quick sync-ups at someone's desk. So saving at least some of those tensions up for a disciplined weekly tactical meeting can free up valuable time and attention.

The tactical meeting

The tactical meeting is a weekly meeting that focuses on the circle's day-to-day work. Although most of the work gets done by roles using their authority and autonomy, they are not isolated islands. Roles need to work together to achieve the circle's goals. The purpose of the tactical meeting, therefore, is to sync up regularly and effectively, so that everyone can move forward with their work. The tactical meeting has a very different format from the governance meeting and moves much faster. On average, it takes about an hour. At the end of it, everyone knows exactly how the circle is doing and what needs to be done next.

Similar to the governance meeting, the agenda for the

tactical meeting is built on the spot and based on tensions. The difference is that these tensions are processed in a much more practical and operational manner. The tactical meeting takes the circle's roles and policies as a given, and instead focuses on the circle's projects, results, progress, and next-actions.

At the tactical meeting, the roles of the circle regularly and rapidly align around the work of the circle

The tactical meeting is not the place to solve each tension there and then. You might compare it to a hospital's emergency room: you've got all kinds of issues coming in, but not everything is equally urgent or important. What you definitely do *not* want to do is take an entire team of specialists to move from patient to patient haphazardly to treat them on the spot or even perform surgery on them! Yet, that is what we often do in meetings. We try to solve problems on the spot, with everyone there.

The tactical meetings in Holacracy are more similar to how an emergency room *actually* works. Every patient is briefly examined to determine how serious the problem is and what is needed to solve it. The majority of patients are not treated on the spot but are referred to the right type of specialist for treatment. The same thing happens in the tactical meeting: tensions are briefly examined and then referred to the role that has the authority and accountability to do what is needed.

Like the governance meeting, the tactical meeting is also led by the Facilitator role. It is his or her job to make sure that *all* agenda items are processed within the allotted time. The Secretary captures any next-actions and projects coming out of the tactical meeting.

The tactical meeting is not the place to discuss the circle's roles and accountabilities; any tensions about those are held until the next governance meeting. Separating these two meetings (tactical and governance) creates a lot of clarity. Mixing these two types of conversation means having neither of them well.

The purpose of the tactical meeting is to process each and every tension within the allotted time and to clarify the next-action for each

Once you get the hang of the governance meeting and the circle has clear roles, you will find that the tactical meetings become a lot easier. It's obvious what roles are needed to solve a given tension, and much easier and faster to identify the next-action. At the same time, the tactical meeting also helps surface any gaps or lack of clarity in the circle's roles and accountabilities, which can then be processed in the next governance meeting. This constant interaction between the governance meeting and the tactical meeting creates ever-more clarity and effectiveness for the circle.

6.2 THE TACTICAL MEETING FORMAT

Like the governance meeting, the tactical meeting has a pre-de-fined format, which is enforced by the Facilitator role. The format is as follows:

- Check-in
- Checklist review
- Metrics review
- Project updatesAgenda-building
- Processing agenda items
- —Item 1
- —Item 2
- —Etc.
- Check-out

Building a shared picture of the circle's current reality

The tactical meeting opens with a check-in round. The purpose of this round is to share what's on your mind, so that you can be fully present for the tactical meeting. The next three rounds (checklist review, metrics review, and project updates) aim to rapidly build a shared picture of how the circle is doing. Doing this every week increases awareness about how the circle as a whole performs. This helps circle members identify tensions early on, so that ad-justments can be made right away.

The first part of the tactical meeting aims to generate a shared picture of the circle's current reality

After the check-in, in the "checklist review" step, the Facilitator runs through a list of recurring tasks one by one (if any are defined—if not, go on to the metrics review). Every checklist item is owned by a role and has a fixed frequency. An example of a checklist item could be "Weekly newsletter sent." This recurring task is done by the Online role, which did indeed send that newsletter this week, and therefore answers "check."Another example of a common checklist item is the weekly review, which is a recurring task for all circle members. Some tasks may also have a different frequency, such as every month or every quarter. The goal in this step is to create transparency on recurring tasks so that they become a habit.

During the checklist review, a question may arise or someone may sense a tension, for example, because someone says they didn't complete a particular task ("no check"). Unlike most meetings, this does not get discussed on the spot, but is captured as an agenda item to come back to later in the meeting (when processing the agenda items). The Facilitator cuts off any discussion or reactions immediately, suggesting to hold them for the agenda as tensions.

The same applies to the next step, which looks at the circle's metrics. The purpose of this "metrics review" is to create a shared picture of the circle's current reality. Are we on the right track? Are we achieving our goals? By looking at a number of relevant metrics regularly, the circle gets a better sense of how things are progressing. What kind of metrics these are depends on the circle's purpose and the type of work that is being done.

Examples of possible metrics include the number of website hits, the percentage of staff illness, or the number of new contracts. Some metrics are reported weekly, while others might get looked at only once a month or every quarter.

During the first part of the tactical meeting, questions and discussion are immediately cut off by the Facilitator

A metric is always connected to a role, which prepares the metric and reports on it at the tactical meeting. By regularly reviewing its metrics over a longer period of time, the circle develops a feel for trends, and starts to become more sensitive to tensions. In the metrics review round, like before, any tensions are held for later discussion as agenda items. This helps keep this round fast, so that there will be enough time later in the meeting to process all agenda items.

The last step before moving on to agenda-building is the "project updates." Here, everyone briefly reports any changes in their current projects. This is more specific than the more common 'status updates': what specifically has changed in this project since the last tactical meeting (usually last week)? The Facilitator asks everyone to report changes on their role's current projects. If nothing changed in a particular project in the past week, then there is no need for a general update, let alone a lengthy explanation of why not. Instead, it is enough just to say "no changes." If anyone senses a tension around this, then that can be added to the agenda in the next step.

The purpose of this step is to give a high-level overview of the circle's work and to get full transparency on what everyone is working on and what progress is being made. In addition, it helps create clarity on each circle member's priorities by seeing which projects they mark as "current" for the coming week. Many circles choose to use a physical board to support this step, but we will come back to that later.

The project updates step gives transparency on what each circle member is working on, what progress is being made, and what his or her priorities are

It is important to keep the updates during the projects round short and concise and to limit the number of ongoing projects. If you don't, the round will slide back into long monologues, losing everyone's attention, and leaving less time for discussing actual agenda items. There is only way to strike the right balance: try it for a few weeks! Just like in the previous rounds, there is no discussion during this step. The goal is to quickly get a high-level overview of where the circle is at. Doing so often highlights gaps between where the circle is now and where it could be or needs to be, which are saved as tensions for the agenda.

Collecting and processing agenda items

After the project updates comes agenda-building. Any circle member can bring tensions to the meeting, and the previous rounds often surface a few more. For example, someone may sense a tension about the number of website hits last week (resulting from the metrics review), and about the lack of progress on two important projects (resulting from the project updates). During agenda-building there is no need to explain each tension; one or two keywords will suffice to add them to the agenda. The Facilitator builds a list of tensions on the spot, including the name or initials of the owner of each tension.

The agenda for the tactical meeting is built on the spot and based on tensions, which are then processed one at a time, within the allotted time

If several people bring a similar, or even the same agenda item (for example, "website visitors"), they are simply added to the agenda multiple times, each time with a different owner. The underlying principle in processing agenda items is: one tension at a time, from one person at a time. When you combine several people's related tensions and discuss them together, chances are you will fail to address any of them well. You are likely, instead, to get into a struggle about what is most important and what would be the "best", most comprehensive solution. Counterintuitively, it turns out to be much quicker to process the same tension multiple times, each time focusing on what one person (the "owner" of the tension) senses and what he or she needs in order to move forward. Rather than slowing things down, this practice actually speeds things up while at the same time leading to better outcomes!

Once the agenda has been created, you start to go down the list one tension at a time. Every agenda item has a single owner. Whether there are three or fifteen items on the agenda, the objective of the tactical meeting is process all of them within the allotted time (most often an hour). Processing agenda items consists of the following steps:

1. The Facilitator asks, "What do you need?" The owner of the agenda item explains.
2. The owner engages with other roles/people as needed

3. The Secretary captures any accepted requests for next-actions or projects
4. The Facilitator asks, "Did you get what you need?"

The Facilitator opens each agenda item by asking the owner what the tension is and what he or she needs. After a brief explanation, the owner can engage other people in or out of their roles. Depending on how much time is available, the Facilitator at some point moves on by asking: "What is the next-action here?" Sometimes it is useful to also capture a project by defining the desired outcome. Next-actions and projects are captured by the Secretary, along with the people and roles that accepted them.

The output of the tactical meeting is a list of next-actions and projects, each assigned to the right role and person

The tactical meeting ends with a check-out, giving everyone a chance to share a brief reflection on the tactical meeting and how it went. The Facilitator makes sure people don't interrupt each other.

6.3 THE PROJECT BOARD

The project board is a visual management tool that provides an overview of the circle's ongoing projects. It lists the projects that the members of the circle want to keep each other informed about. By maintaining and reporting on it every week, the circle is able to keep track of important ongoing work. This creates a high level of transparency about the circle's overall progress and priorities, so that any tensions can be identified early on.

Creating the project board

To create a project board you need a large, empty surface, like a white board or a wall, in the room where the circle does its tactical meetings. Some teams prefer a digital project board, which is then projected during the weekly tactical meeting. The project board is a simple grid, in which the rows refer to the roles and the columns refer to the project status. You will have as many rows as there are roles in the circle, and four columns; one for each project status.

The project board provides an at-a-glance overview of the circle's most relevant, ongoing projects

Each project can only have one owner and one status; it must always fall clearly within one row and one column on the project board. Each project is formulated as a desired outcome and is linked to a role. If a project falls outside of any defined roles, then it is an "individual action."

The project board includes a selection of the most relevant ongoing projects of the circle; it is *not* intended to be a complete overview of all of the circle's projects! There are two reasons why a project may be added to the project board. The first one is that the owner decides that it is relevant for the rest of the circle and must therefore be added. The other reason is that someone makes a request to add a particular project to the project board in order to more easily track its progress.

A project can have one of four statuses: "current," "waiting," "done," or "future." Current projects are projects that you will be working on in the coming week (until the next tactical meeting). If you can't continue with a project because you are waiting for something or someone, this project will get the "waiting" status. This always concerns an external factor: someone else has to do something, or you can only continue after a certain event has taken place. The project status "done" speaks for itself: the desired outcome has been achieved. Projects with the status "future" are projects that you intend to work on, but not in the coming week. You could see this as the "backlog" of projects from which you will "pull" from week to week.

The project board in practice

In practice, projects are always moving around the project board. They often start out with a "future" status, at some point are activated ("current"), and eventually move to the "done" column. Some projects end up in the "waiting" column for a while, and then become "current" again once you have an answer or the relevant event has taken place.

The more effectively the circle functions, the faster projects will move across the project board will be. You can even measure a circle's "velocity" by assigning a relative score to each project (for example, one to five stars) and then counting the number of units (stars) the circle completes per week.

The weekly review (your "meeting with yourself") is a great time to update your own projects on the project board. You make a conscious choice about what you will be working on this week (current), and which projects you won't (future). You will likely need to move some projects from the "current" column to "waiting" or to "done". Others will move from "waiting" back to "current," or perhaps to "done."

Based on the updated project board, the circle builds a shared picture of its progress and priorities. This happens in the project updates round in the tactical meeting, where each circle member reports on the changes in each of their current projects. Remember: these are not general status updates, but very specific reports about what changed since the previous tactical meeting (or, "No change" if nothing changed).

The project board generates transparency on everyone's progress and priorities

After the project updates, everyone knows exactly what the others are working on and how they are prioritizing their attention among their ongoing projects. Often, tensions are surfaced about a specific project's progress or priority. These are immediately added to the tactical meeting's agenda, so that the circle can sync up and identify a next-action. In this way, you don't have to wait until something is done before you raise a tension, but instead you can track progress and make adjustments almost continuously. For optimal use of the project board, it is important that only a *selection* of projects are added to it. If everyone adds all of their projects, the overview will soon be lost and just doing the project updates will take half an hour or more. Only add projects to the board that others need to know about or that were specifically requested by someone. These projects are all formulated as desired outcomes, like "April newsletter sent out" or "Database cleaned up." If it concerns bigger, long-term projects, you may want to break them up into smaller projects. That way the project updates round stays interesting and relevant.

6.4 FACILITATOR AND SECRETARY

The quality of the tactical meeting is strongly tied to the clarity and discipline with which it is led. Just like at the governance meeting, this is the Facilitator's job, although the format of the tactical meeting is very different. The heart of it is building an agenda based on tensions, and processing them into clear next-actions and projects one by one. These outputs are recorded and distributed by the Secretary.

Facilitating the tactical meeting

The Facilitator opens the meeting with a check-in, as is usual in Holacracy. The check-in is followed by three rounds that are intended as quick update rounds to gain insight into how the circle is doing: the checklist review, metrics review, and project updates. The focus in each of these rounds is on sharing information, so reactions and discussions are not permitted. If someone begins to react or engage another in discussion, the Facilitator cuts him or her off immediately. Clarifying questions are allowed, but anything else is saved for later by adding it to the agenda. The purpose of these three rounds is to surface relevant tensions for the agenda.

> *The facilitator immediately cuts off any reactions or discussion until it is time to build the agenda. Tensions are added to the agenda so that they can be discussed later in the meeting.*

Once an agenda has been built, the Facilitator uses two principles to engage with it:

1. Process all agenda items within the allotted time.
2. Process one tension at a time, from one person at a time.

Whether it's 45 or 60 minutes, the Facilitator ensures that all agenda items are processed within the time set for the meeting. The order in which items are processed isn't particularly important, because everything will get addressed anyway. The Facilitator opens each agenda item by asking the owner: "What do you need?" After the owner of the tension answers that questions, there is space to engage other roles and people. The Facilitator plays a crucial role here, particularly in the beginning stages of implementing Holacracy. If people are getting referenced by name, the Facilitator may step in to clarify which role is being addressed. The tactical meeting is the ideal place to begin practice role awareness. What role has the authority to make a decision here? From which of my various roles do I sense this tension? Why am I directing my question to you? What is it that we expect from each other, and do our current governance records give us the right to expect that? If not, we have an opportunity to create more clarity by bringing a proposal to the circle's next governance meeting (rather than have the discussion here, during the tactical meeting). It is the Facilitator's job to constantly listen for the connection between the circle's day-to-day work and its current roles and accountabilities. Each agenda item is processed by clarifying what is needed, and what the next-action is. If necessary, in addition to next-actions, projects may also be requested. The Secretary captures those requests for next-actions and projects that are accepted, including the roles and persons who have accepted them.

The Facilitator makes sure that all agenda items are processed one by one within the allotted time and always with a clear owner

Meanwhile, the Facilitator makes sure that enough time is left to treat the remaining agenda items. If there is little time, you focus more on what the next-action is. If it is not clear enough yet what the tension is, or what is needed to address it, then the next-action may also be to schedule a short follow-up meeting with the relevant roles. This way, even an agenda of twenty tensions can be completed within the allotted time.

The purpose of the tactical meeting is not to solve all the tensions there and then, but to track progress and remove obstacles, so that everyone can move forward with their work. Discussing everything in detail and as a group is not only inefficient, but it also contradicts the principle of distributed authority: everyone is an entrepreneur in his or her roles, with the authority to make any decision or take any action needed to move them forward.

Having a good Secretary and Facilitator provides a huge boost to the quality of the meeting and the meeting outputs. In a high-performing circle, all they do is remind participants of the rules now and then, because by then everyone knows exactly what is expected of them and can focus on simply "playing the game."

The purpose of the tactical meeting is not to solve everything on the spot, but to track progress by identifying and assigning clear next-actions and projects

ALIGNMENT

John has asked for everyone to be in the boardroom at nine o'clock that morning. Just after nine, Soraya, Will, Neil, and Suzanne are standing in front of the project board with John. When Suzanne moves to sit down, John asks her to stay standing up.

"This meeting is done standing up, to keep it short."

Suzanne sighs. "Okay, good to know. Next time I won't wear my heels."

John takes the floor. "Today I'll introduce a different type of operational meeting, called the daily stand-up."

He goes on to explain that the stand-up consists of a check-in and a quick round of updates.

Will looks at the project board. "That sounds a lot like a tactical meeting. What's the difference?"

John replies, "The difference is, first of all that it is daily, rather than weekly. Secondly, it is very short; ten to fifteen minutes tops. We also don't do any of the rounds we do in the tactical meeting, like the metrics review. You can think of it more as a safety net between the weekly tactical meetings and your own daily work. It helps us make sure that nothing falls between the cracks.

Soraya asks, "But is it really necessary to do it every day?"

John tells her, "The stand-up is an optional meeting, not like the tactical meeting, which is essential. But if you decide to do this, it works best if you do it every day."

Another question from Soraya, "Does it matter that Lien and

Tamara are not here for it?"

"It is too bad they're not here, but it is worth the effort even if not everyone is there. I would recommend doing it every day at exactly the same time and place; then you have the best chance of it becoming a habit. Having the project board around helps a lot, too."

After they have done their check-in, they move on to the updates round. John explains that there are three questions to answer here: "What did you get done yesterday? What do you intend to get done today? And is there anything you need?"

Neil says, "That's it?"

"Yes, that's all there is to it. It is very simple, really."

Neil smiles. "I'm realizing that I do this every day, except I do it just with myself and my own lists."

Everyone laughs.

John tells him, "So, Neil, now you get to do it with us."

Neil tells them that tomorrow he has to do a presentation about the campaign budget and that he needs input from everyone today. "I sent out an email about that yesterday." Next, he hears from Will and Suzanne that they are going to be out of the office all day today.

"When will you two be able to give me that input?" he asks them.

"I'll try to do it in a little while," Suzanne says.

○

The stand-up really does take less than fifteen minutes. Neil is in good spirits when he walks back to his desk. He knows what most of the team will be working on today. He had been thinking of a number of emails that he was planning to send, but now he longer needs to. This could really save him a lot of time. And he will probably have a much better sense of when something is about to go off the rails. An unanswered email today can sometimes become a problem only much later on. For the first time, he can see how the tactical meeting and stand-up help him to stay on top of the circle's work.

But, when Neil checks his email later that day, Suzanne's input is still not there. The presentation is tomorrow morning. He takes a deep breath and wonders how to come up with those figures before then. The TV campaign is the biggest part of the overall campaign budget. There is no point in giving a presentation without it.

Because of the tactical meeting and the stand-up, he knows much more about what everyone is doing, but at the same time, it frustrates him that he can't force the information out of them. Is Holacracy going to solve that problem for him? What do you do when someone doesn't live up to their basic responsibilities?

He stands up to go get a cup of coffee. Should he be honest and tell Rakesh that he doesn't have all the information he needs, or should he just bluff his way through?

When he is back behind his desk he checks his and Rakesh's calendars. Maybe something has changed? No, it doesn't look like it. The presentation is definitely scheduled for tomorrow. He already postponed it once and he doesn't want to do it again. And anyway, they need management approval to move on to the next phase of the campaign.

He decides to call Rakesh's secretary to ask if the presentation can be moved to late morning; that way he'll still have time to get what he needs first thing in the morning.

6.5 DAILY STAND-UP

The stand-up is a daily meeting of about ten to fifteen minutes, in which the circle seeks rapid alignment about its work and any tensions that have come up. To keep the meeting short and focused, it is done standing up, hence the name. The stand-up often takes place in the morning so the group can start the day together.

If you don't do a stand-up to "save time", you often end up spending more time on all kinds of "short" interruptions, emails, and impromptu meetings at the coffee machine. Taking those few minutes every morning can actually save you a lot of time throughout the day.

This type of meeting works best for teams that work closely together and speak to each other a lot, whether in person or by email. Unlike the circle's tactical and governance meetings, the daily stand-up is optional. Try it for at least a week or two before you decide if you want to make a habit of it!

The daily stand-up can save time by rapidly aligning with each other at the start of the day in a short, structured meeting about the circle's work

The structure of the stand-up is simple:
- Check-in
- Updates

Like every meeting in Holacracy, the stand-up starts with a check-in. Because the meeting is so short and you do it every day, the check-in should be short and sweet, too. How are you feeling today and what has your attention? After the check-in, everyone gives a quick update, in a round. You can use different formats for this, but the next three questions are a great way to get started:

- What did you get done yesterday?
- What do you intend to get done today?
- Do you need anything?

The aim of the updates round is to create transparency on what everyone is working on—not to micro-manage each other, but to give you the necessary information to move forward with your own work. This is one of the best ways to build strong ties between team members. After the round of updates the stand-up is over, but you may find people often linger to immediately address some of the tensions that were surfaced during the stand-up. This is a great example of the principle of slowing down at first, so you can speed up later!

SEVEN

DISTRIBUTED LEADERSHIP

FRICTION

The next morning Neil still has not received anything from Suzanne. She also failed to attend the stand-up. When he walks into her office, she is typing on her phone.

"Do you have a minute?" he asks.

She doesn't respond. Did she not hear him?

"Do you have a minute?" Neil asks again.

"I can hear you, I'm not deaf. I just have to finish this text, okay?" Suzanne snaps.

Neil waits.

"Okay. What's up?"

Neil says, "Can you give me the overview that I've been asking you for for the last few days now?"

"Sorry, but I've been really busy."

Neil's tone is urgent. "I really need it *now*. I have to do the presentation today."

Suzanne scrolls down her emails. "Looks like I didn't get the figures from the ad agency yet."

Neil takes a deep breath. *Stay calm now.*

"Suzanne, this is not the first time I've asked you for something and not gotten it from you. I need to be able to count on some basic responsibilities, just like with everyone else."

Suzanne's eyebrows go up in mock surprise. "Oh, it's all very nice, those basic responsibilities, Holacracy and what-not, but I have a North American campaign to run and our regional campaigns are still ongoing."

Neil sighs. "We're all busy, Suzanne. But do you at least have some kind of overview of your projects and expenses for me?"

"Listen, if I had to follow up on your requests for information all the time, I'd never get around to doing any actual work. I know what I'm doing here."

Neil is annoyed now. "Maybe you do, but I'm completely in the dark here." Then, more calmly, he says, "It's all in your head, which is hardly transparent."

Suzanne replies, fiercely, "Now, you listen to me! I've been in this business for nearly ten years and I've never been treated this way. Being constantly harassed like this. I sent you some stuff last week, didn't I? Can't you figure it out from looking at that?"

Neil, quietly "That was not complete. Every time I need something from you, I have to to chase you for it. You keep everything to yourself. What, we should all be accountable except for you?"

"You know what? If you want to keep nagging, be my guest. I've had it. Ever since the last reorganization, things have been going downhill. I don't give a damn about your figures."

Suzanne stalks out of the room, leaving Neil speechless.

○

Neil feels a headache coming on as he walks back to his desk. If Suzanne were to quit, they would all be in a lot of trouble. What would he say to Rakesh and Denis? That they can't handle the project after all? That two months in, it has spun out of control? Or that he can not get a grip on his team? No, that is not an option.

Suzanne is a professional; she knows a lot of people in the industry and she is well-respected. He needs her in order to pull this off. But she's just impossible to work with. They were just starting to get things under control with the meeting rhythm. Where did it go wrong?

Neil stares at his computer screen. The clock says it's already ten. One hour until the presentation. What to do? Maybe John has an idea. He picks up the phone and punches in his number.

"Hi John, have you got a minute? Great. I just had a big fight with Suzanne and now it looks like the campaign might go belly-up. Is there anything in Holacracy that can help me solve this?"

John doesn't say anything, and for a moment Neil wonders if he lost the connection. Then he says, "To be honest, Neil, Holacracy doesn't solve every problem. It just surfaces problems that were already there, so that you can deal with them. It's not a golden bullet."

Alarmed, Neil says, "So I'm on my own here?"

"Look, what just happened between you and Suzanne would have happened without Holacracy too. It would have just taken a little longer."

Neil gets up and walks over to the window. "My understanding was that Holacracy helps the team to resolve its own conflicts. Well, that's not happening, is it?"

John calmly answers, "It's not that easy, Neil. If you fill a role, such as the Lead Link in your case, and you sense a tension, then you have to take responsibility, to be accountable ... If you think you can just sit back and let the system do the work, well, don't hold your breath."

Neil lets the words sink in. "Are you saying I have to show leadership?"

John counters, "I'm not sure exactly what you mean by that."

"Well, I mean confront Suzanne."

"That is one way of looking at leadership. But that way, you make it personal."

"What do you mean?"

"Okay, for example, you're talking about 'my problem' and 'I had a fight.' When you talk that way, you're falling into the trap of heroic leadership. Remember the talk we had about that?"

"That you take it all on your shoulders."

"Exactly."

"But this is different. This is something between Suzanne and me!"

John says, "No, what I'm telling you is that it isn't. You sense a tension because you fill a certain role. If you didn't fill that role, you probably would not have clashed with Suzanne."

"That's probably true. Before I became a manager, we got along pretty well. I used to really enjoy working with her."

"But now, from your role as Lead Link, you definitely have a responsibility to do something about this tension. This is something you can't afford to ignore."

"All right. So now what?"

"What I'm saying is: process your tension."

ACCOUNTABILITY

ater that morning, Neil is about to start his presentation to upper management about the North American campaign's progress to date. He feels nervous, because he needs their approval on the budgets and Rakesh has a tendency to ask very detailed questions. He connects his laptop with the beamer so he can get started. Rakesh looks at his watch.

"We don't have a lot of time, Neil, so I hope you can bring us up to speed quickly."

After the second slide, Rakesh starts to fire off his questions. "What are the ad agency's deliverables, and how do you intend to keep the budget under control?"

Neil feels a knot in his stomach. He keeps his eyes on his notes and explains how complicated the integration between the various channels is, and how this campaign is different from the ones they usually run.

Rakesh looks at him sternly. "I'm sure it is, but that does not answer my question."

"I'm still waiting for the last figures …" Neil tries to avoid Rakesh's gaze. He wants to say that Suzanne is not cooperating, but he swallows his words at the last moment. He doesn't want to make excuses.

Rakesh says, "Well, it looks like you're not quite on top of things, Neil. That's not what I expected, not from you. I want you to go back to your team and make sure that you can bring us the necessary figures by next week. I'm sure you can understand that we can't continue without them."

○

Back at his desk, Neil has trouble concentrating; he feels tense all over. Everything seems to be coming unhinged. This whole thing is turning into a real disaster! He goes to get a cup of coffee and walks over to the window. The rain is coming down in sheets.

He doesn't want to continue covering for Suzanne. But what then? They're too far into the campaign to give up. Suzanne works how she has always worked: creative, yet also chaotic. It doesn't look like she is willing to change that. But it's starting to cause some real problems for them.

At the same time, her expertise is important to the team. Until now, he had always considered it his job to protect his team members, which often meant solving problems for them. Now he recalls what John said earlier today—that if this is a tension for his role, then he is accountable to do something about it. But what? Threaten to fire her, slash her bonus, start a file on her? How does he get someone to do something they don't want to do?

Okay, stop thinking like a manager for a minute. You are the Lead Link, Neil.

He sits down at his desk again and looks up the description of the Lead Link. One of the role's accountabilities is: "Assigning roles to people, monitoring the fit, offering feedback to enhance the fit, and re-assigning roles to other people when useful for enhancing fit." There it is, it's very clear. He takes a deep breath and at last begins to calm down: he knows what he has to do now.

7.1 LEADERSHIP IN HOLACRACY

Neil is struggling. As the manager, he carried final responsibility for the team's performance and for "his" people. He is still getting a feel for his new role of Lead Link: what is expected of him now and what isn't anymore? And what does it even mean to be a "Lead Link"? What kind of a leader is he supposed to be?

Leadership: it is one of the hardest and simultaneously one of the most important topics in the shift to Holacracy.

First of all, the word means something different in Holacracy than it does in conventional organizations. The word "leadership" generally refers to a set of personal traits. It is often distinguished from "management," where the focus is more on control. In contrast to management, leadership can also be displayed outside of a formal position or role, in a more personal capacity.

In Holacracy, it is exactly the other way around: leadership is intimately connected to roles. And not just with one centralized role, like that of team leader or manager. Instead, authority is distributed to well-defined roles in the governance meeting. This creates a set-up that could be described as "distributed leadership." Not only the manager, but everyone exercises leadership, each within their roles and accountabilities. Leadership in Holacracy is therefore by definition "role leadership."

In Holacracy, leadership is distributed: everyone exercises leadership within their roles and accountabilities

But what about being a leader *outside* of your roles? In conventional organizations, this is considered the essence of leadership: taking responsibility, even (or in particular) where it cannot be formally expected or asked for. This kind of "heroic behavior" is generally viewed as positive. It is seen as a sign that you are highly involved and have "passion for the company."From a holacratic perspective however, this type of behavior comes with a cost: every time you take individual action (action outside of your roles), you rob the organization of an opportunity to create more clarity in a more enduring, structural way, rather than personally and temporarily. It is apparently unclear who is accountable for dealing with a certain problem, so you take it on. This will make the tension go away for a while, until something similar happens and it is again unclear who's accountable for dealing with this tension.

Of course, solving problems and helping the organization are good things. There is nothing wrong with individual action. But if it becomes a pattern, something you do regularly, then you are falling into the trap of "heroic leadership." This type of leadership runs counter to Holacracy's role leadership. Instead, it may be better to say, "Not my role," and bring the tension to the next governance meeting. Depending on how urgent the tension is, there is no reason you cannot take individual action to resolve it in the short term. But by bringing it to the governance meeting, you make sure that you also resolve it in the long term, by clarifying which role is accountable. This removes the need for heroic leadership, because it is now part of the circle's role structure. Yes, leadership is still required, but now it is embedded in a clear, ongoing role!

Heroic leadership runs counter to distributed leadership because it deprives the organization of the opportunity to create more structural role clarity

Leadership and the Lead Link

You may be wondering how all that fits in with the Lead Link role. After all, it has the word "lead" in it. So isn't it just another way of saying "supervisor" or "manager"? This is a hard question to answer. Yes, the Lead Link leads the circle. And, no, the Lead Link does not manage or supervise the people in the circle. In Holacracy, we distinguish between roles and the people filling those roles, as well as between a circle and a team. A circle consists of roles; a team consists of people. Building on this distinction, the Lead Link does not lead the people and the team, but rather, the circle within which people lead their own roles. This is a subtle, but crucial, difference that constitutes a paradigm shift from how we conventionally look at leadership.

The Lead Link does not lead the people, but rather, the circle within which people lead their own roles

Leadership is distributed from managers into well-defined roles with real authority. Everyone now exercises leadership, except they lead their roles and themselves, not other people. The Lead Link's job is to create the conditions so that people can lead their roles, in service of the circle's purpose.

The Lead Link determines who will be in the circle and, if need be, can also remove people from the circle. This is not the same as hiring and firing people: those are accountabilities that can be defined and assigned to a specific role. You might for example bring a proposal to the governance meeting to create a People role that does that. Whatever you do, keep in mind that unlike a manager, the Lead Link can never be accountable for hiring, firing, evaluating, and rewarding people.

When people lead their roles and the circle performs well, the Lead Link is happy. In fact, it will likely take very little time to fill the role, because the Lead Link does not do any operational work for the circle. Keep in mind that the *person* filling the Lead Link role may fill other, operational roles in the circle, in which case that person does do operational work – but not from her Lead Link role!

Another way of looking at it is that the Lead Link constantly strives to make herself redundant, by enabling the circle to work autonomously from their roles.For a former manager, the Lead Link role may take some getting used to. It is more a process of unlearning than of learning, especially when it comes to a manager's tendency to "take care" of "her" people, and to motivate and manage those who are now self-managing. In the beginning, a Lead Link will really have to learn to hold back and let go. Later it will become clear that some type of direction is actually needed from the Lead Lead, but one that's focused on the circle's work and not on the people and the team. The Lead Link therefore plays a key role (for better or for worse) in the transformation from conventional to distributed leadership.

SHOCK

The next morning, Neil speaks to Suzanne.

"I'll just get right to the point," he says, when they sit down across from each other. He tells her about his disastrous presentation to management. "I felt like a total fool yesterday."

Suzanne's face starts to turn red.

Neil continues confidently, "Look Suzanne, we, all of us together, have started to do things differently. That may be inconvenient for you, but offering some basic transparency is a part of that."

"Oh, great. Now you're going to lecture me about those damn roles again?"

Neil takes a deep breath. "The way you run your role makes it hard to do mine. And that means we're not achieving our circle's goals."

"I know exactly what I'm working on."

"It's not about that, Suzanne. You are really good at what you do; I'm not questioning that in any way. But you keep all the information to yourself. If I need anything from you, I have to ask for it several times before I get it. That is just not workable."

"I don't know ...," Suzanne begins hesitantly. "Something has really changed since the last reorganization. Before that we weren't so obsessed with numbers. Now we're spending half our time reporting."

"Last year the stakes weren't as high," Neil tells her. "There was enough money; the sky was the limit. But as you are well aware, it's just not like that anymore. There are major opportunities for us in the market right now, but we have to be much faster to be able to seize them. Just a few months from now, we have to deliver some spectacular results."

"Sorry, Neil, but now I need to say something. Ever since you've become a manager, things have started to go wrong. We used to be a tight-knit team; we were ready to take on the world. Now we're sitting around having meetings all the time, talking about circles and roles, and nothing is happening. ... To tell you the truth, I'm just not enjoying it anymore."

"What do you mean?"

"Okay, first you came up with that capacity plan. Which, by the way, I never participated in. And then you change all the meetings and I have to justify myself to the entire team."

"It's not about justifying yourself; all we need is some basic transparency about what you are working on. That's not the same thing."

"It doesn't work that way, Neil. I have never worked that way. What you want me to do, that's just not me." Suzanne takes a deep breath and looks at Neil. For a moment he has a glimpse of the energetic, creative Suzanne he used to have such great talks with, after work, in the pub.

"There is something I need to tell you. ... I haven't really made a decision yet. Or maybe I have. I got an offer to work on a film production in Atlanta. For a friend of mine. She runs her own company. It's something I've always dreamed of."

Neil is taken aback. "But what about our campaign?"

"Well, I thought about that, of course. But ... I haven't been happy here for some time. It's nothing personal."

"Sorry?"

"It's not going to do anyone any good if I stay here just feeling frustrated all the time."

"You want to leave?"

"To be perfectly honest, yes, I do."

"You mean right away?"

"They've already started filming."

"So you're leaving immediately!"

"If I could, I would fly to Georgia this week."

○

Neil grabs his jacket and walks out of the office, toward the waterfront. He quit smoking years ago, but he wouldn't mind a cigarette now. Stupid of him not to have seen this coming. Man, this couldn't be happening at a worse time. The preparation for the campaign is just going into the last phase now. They have another month and a half to get everything in place and they are running behind schedule as it is.

What should he do?

His mind is all over the place. Blow off the whole thing? No, impossible. Quit his job? And miss the greatest opportunity of his career? No, absolutely not. Force Suzanne to stay? That wouldn't accomplish much. And the way she works is definitely a problem. Hire a new Suzanne? That could work, but where do you find someone with that much experience, and on such short notice?

He is getting angry, thinking about Suzanne going her own way and letting him down. But then he is reminded of what John said, about the difference between the role and the person. Part of him can see where she's coming from. Suzanne has always been attracted to the glamour of film and television. It's her thing. The fact that she has other roles and accountabilities that she is much less interested in has only become more visible lately, because of Holacracy.

As Lead Link, Neil feels some serious tension. He can physically feel it in his stomach. Should he jump in and take over her work himself? He quickly dismisses that thought. He already works more hours than is good for him.

After five minutes of brisk walking, he starts to calm down. He takes out his phone, calls John and begins explaining the situation to him. But before he has a chance to finish, John interrupts him. "You'll need to keep it short, Neil. I'm about to go into a meeting."

"... I'm wondering how to find a new Suzanne," Neil exclaims in desperation.

"You're asking the wrong question."

"What do you mean?"

"Don't make it so personal. Think roles."

"I don't get it."

"Just take a good look at the roles she fills before you rush into hiring anyone. ... I've got to go now. We'll talk later, sorry." And John hangs up.

"Think roles, right ..." Neil mutters under his breath as he walks back to the office. When he's sitting behind his computer again he opens the web page where the team keeps track of its roles. He clicks on the overview and then on Suzanne. A list of her roles appears on the screen. Just looking at it calms him down already. Yes, of course, as Lead Link he has the authority to assign the team's roles and reassign them if necessary. But how does he do that? Call a meeting? Maybe. He looks at the screen again and imagines the roles as hats, each in a different color. He writes each role's name down on a Post-it note and starts moving them around on his desk. He feels a childish delight, as if he were working on a puzzle. A sudden smile lights up his face. Yes! This might just work!

7.2 IS HOLACRACY FOR EVERYONE?

Holacracy offers a lot of freedom, but it is not without responsibility. Holacracy can bring clarity about expectations and increased speed and productivity. It is flexible enough to work in many different industries and contexts. But that does not mean that Holacracy is a good fit for every organization, for every team, and certainly not for every individual, as has become clear from the interaction between Neil and Suzanne. Holacracy's essence is best summed up in the idea of distributed authority. The manager is no longer the central authority that determines what everyone should do, and how.

Instead, accountability and authority are now distributed in well-defined roles in regular governance meetings. When you energize a role, you get to make decisions about the way in which you fulfill your accountabilities. No one else can tell you how to do your work, including the Lead Link.

What you *can* do as Lead Link (or anyone else) is request transparency from a role about what they're working on, what the current status is, and what the role's priorities look like. And everyone, including the Lead Link, can bring proposals to the governance meeting, in order to change or clarify what can be expected from a role. If you are used to the manager having the final say, Holacracy will be a real shock to the system. If you are a manager, then it comes down to letting go—literally letting go and not just delegating, but truly distributing accountability and authority, Letting go of control, trusting that Holacracy will offer you new ways of exercising leadership. Perhaps it is really the *illusion* of control that you have to give up, and you gain another kind of control in its place. The kind that is based on transparency, so that you always know just how the circle is doing and which allows you to change course much easier and earlier.

If you are not a manager, then the challenge is to really own and lead the roles you have taken on. In addition to accountability, you now have full authority to make decisions about how you energize your role. What results do you want to achieve? What are your priorities? Where do you start and what do you need from others? In Holacracy, it's much harder to hide, whether behind your manager, your colleagues, or how busy you are. Transparency is a double-edged sword: you have much more insight into what others are working on and what priorities they're setting, but your own progress and priorities are just as visible—and that can be pretty confronting at times.

Distributed authority and transparency are not vague ideas that you should just "have faith" in. They are ground rules, anchored in the Holacracy Constitution. Asking the current powerholder to put a signature under it is not just a ritual; it is literally a transfer of authority to the set of rules outlined in the Constitutuion, and in particular to the circle's governance meeting, where authority is further defined and distributed. Adopting Holacracy transforms the power structure of the team or organization. From then on, Holacracy's ground rules apply and no-one is above the law, including the (former) manager. You can almost compare it to a king or queen voluntarily abdicating their power. A metaphor that is all the more striking if you realize that behind today's organizations' modern facade, there continues to exist a power structure that is eerily similar to the feudal model that in society, we have left far behind us!

ADAPTATION

Neil is in the meeting room with Tamara, Lien, and Will. He tells them that Suzanne has decided to leave them. His colleagues are shocked to hear the news.

"What? She's leaving? When?"

"What happened?"

Neil gives them his side of the story. He takes his time.

"Ultimately, it is her decision," he finishes.

Tamara: "Now that I think about it I'm not really that surprised. She is someone who prefers to do her own thing."

Lien looks worried. "But that does mean we have a problem, don't we? Who is going to take over her work?"

Tamara looks at Neil. "I'm overworked as it is, so I won't be able to take on much more. Couldn't we just hire someone new?"

Neil tells the group, "I thought about that and it's probably what we will end up doing. Except it will easily take a month before we find someone and show them the ropes. So I was thinking, why not try something else?"

Will leans back in his chair. "Well, let's hear it."

Neil explains, "It's my job as Lead Link to figure out the best fit for each of the roles in our circle. So I thought, let's take a look at the current division of roles. I did a bit of prep work already."

He walks over to the wall and sticks on the Post-it notes he had prepared earlier. The others watch him in silence.

"Try to look at these without thinking of the status quo for a minute. What roles are a good fit for you?"

By moving the notes around and having a few short discussions, they come up with a new way of assigning the circle's roles in less than half an hour.

Lien observes, "I'm noticing that Suzanne had a number of roles that she took on primarily because she was doing that type of work before. But she wasn't necessarily the best fit for each of them. For example, I think the PR role goes better with what I do," she says. "In my Copywriter role, I am constantly telling our story already and I'm comfortable enough in front of a camera."

Neil nods his agreement. "I like it, Lien. You're right, it's not just about what someone happens to have taken on, but about making the best possible use of the talent and expertise of the people in our circle."

By the end of the meeting, most of Suzanne's roles have been redistributed among the team; there is just one role left.

Neil says, "I'm thinking we could hire a freelancer to do that. This will really reduce our costs, freeing up a nice chunk of budget for other things."

"Wow, we have really overestimated Suzanne's capacities," Tamara says with a grin. "Or underestimated our own!"

○

After the meeting, Neil feels great relief. It looks like he will not need to hire someone new, at least not in the short run. He wonders how to explain the situation to HR. He's not too worried about Rakesh; as long as they're saving money he will be happy.

Still, he wonders how this will all work out. He hired some of the team members himself, and he put a lot of effort into picking the best people for each position. There were a lot of candidates and a lot of interviews. Now he realizes that he would have been better off focusing on what specific roles were needed, first.

What most surprises him is how he seems to be taking Suzanne's departure in stride. Is it because he doesn't care about her? Because he is only thinking about results? No, that's not it. He wishes the best for her. He was upset at first, because for a moment it seemed like everything was going to fall apart. But now that everything has calmed down, he sincerely hopes she will do well in the film industry.

Although he doesn't always show it, he does care about his team members. This is one of the strange things about Holacracy. On the surface it appears so impersonal, but in reality it creates more space for personal connection, not less. Inspired by the outcome of the meeting, he is beginning to believe that they can pull it off after all.

The week after, the team is swamped with work. Their daily stand-ups and the tactical meeting help them stay on the same page. The update rounds are becoming more and more relevant. Hearing about each other's progress gives them extra motivation to move their own work forward. Their research shows that the campaign does not appeal to all of their targets. They discuss it in the tactical meeting and define a number of next-actions for adjusting the strategy. The launch is just one month away though. Next week Monday, Neil is due to report back to management. He better be prepared: Rakesh really knows how to turn up the heat. ...

THE TURNING POINT

I t is the beginning of June and the temperature has shot up. Summer is in the air. The sidewalk cafes are buzzing with tourists; the wet and cold of the previous months are a distant memory.

Neil takes an afternoon walk along the waterfront. The sun warms his face. When he gets back to the office, his mind is on the presentation he is about to give to the management team. They want to hear about the team's progress on the campaign, and there is a lot at stake. It will be challenging this time.

When everyone is seated around the long conference table, Rakesh opens the meeting.

"Neil, tell us where you are with the campaign."

Neil starts with an overview of the objectives, but before he can get up to steam, Rakesh interrupts him. A rather unpleasant habit, but everyone seems to think it's normal by now.

"I remember the objectives. You told me that the first of July is going to be a problem. Is that still true?"

"Yes. I could go into more detail, but the long and short of it is that we're not going to make it," Neil says.

"Let's account for a week's holiday around the Fourth of July—I think the tenth would still work. At least, that's what I understood from Denis when I last spoke with him. But then I want you to guarantee that we will be able to meet that deadline, and for the entire campaign."

This is what Neil feared. It's just like Rakesh to push a deadline like that. His mind is already made up; now he just wants Neil to confirm the "agreement." How many times have they played this game?

"Rakesh, what I can show you and what I have prepared is a detailed projection of when we think we can launch each region. But I can't give you a solid deadline. If I did that, I would be making myself and you an empty promise. This project has so many moving parts that whatever I tell you now will have to be adjusted again by next week."

Neil looks around the room and sees a lot of frowning. Rakesh laughs uncomfortably.

"You can't be serious. Listen, we made a commitment to Denis. We have millions riding on this. What I need is a hard deadline, not that projection crap."

Neil saw it coming and takes a deep breath. *Don't get baited. Just stay calm.*

"I can't give you a hard deadline."

"Then we have a problem," Rakesh says stiffly.

"If it's a date you want, I can give you one: August first. How's that?"

"Is that a date you're sure of?"

"No, of course I'm not sure."

"Listen, there's no way I can take that to the client. I want you to go back to your team and come back with a hard date."

Rakesh's words linger. No one else says anything. Neil looks at the printout of his presentation, before him on the table. There are some detailed analyses that they have not even looked at; a lot of work went into them. Has the time come to stand up to Rakesh? He clenches his fists and looks Rakesh in the eyes.

"So what is it you want then?"

"Excuse me?"

"These deadlines are just a way of fooling ourselves. We always end up having to adjust them anyway. Is that what you want?" Neil's voice is calmer now.

"Listen, Rakesh, I prepared a presentation that will show you exactly where we are and what the status of each region is. All I ask is that you hear me out."

There's a murmur around the room. Then, with an icy look, Rakesh says, "Okay, let's have it."

For the next half hour, Neil takes them through a detailed analysis of their research results, which shows that the campaign will likely not work in a number of regions, at least not in its current form.

"The briefing that went out to the ad agency earlier was not based on the latest information. It was just something we 'made up,' just like we make up all kinds of things here that have little to do with reality."

"I remember that, but I think it was because we had to move fast." Rakesh looks at his notes. He looks up again when Neil gets to the last slide and wraps up his presentation.

"Thank you. I have to say, I am impressed with your analysis. It paints a clear picture of the campaign, and I believe your projection of August first is realistic. I don't like to go back on my commitments, but I'm willing to give Denis a call and talk it over."

Rakesh grabs his phone and walks out of the boardroom. Five minutes later he is back, looking a little pale: "They won't accept a delay. Not one day."

7.3 DYNAMIC STEERING

It may look as if Neil and Rakesh don't get along very well, but in reality their conflict is not a personal one. The conflict is rather between two different models of management. Rakesh manages according to plans and deadlines, while Neil is increasingly recognizing the power of transparency and making continuous adjustments. In Holacracy, this is called "dynamic steering," and it draws inspiration from the principles of Agile software development.

Traditionally, software was developed by doing a lot of up-front planning and then executing the plan in a highly controlled way. Agile has a completely different approach: you rapidly create a workable first version, which is then tested in the field (for software, this often means letting the end user try it). The feedback generated in this way is used to make immediate adjustments. In this way, you work towards the end result in short cycles, often in less time and at a lower cost.

As many companies are now discovering, you can also use this approach outside of the software world. With Holacracy, you can apply the Agile approach to the organization itself. Instead of designing the organizational structure of circles and roles (Agile calls this "big design upfront"), you rapidly create a workable structure, which you then constantly adjust based on tensions. The same logic applies to the way circles and roles produce results: rapid, workable solutions that are continuously adjusted.

Dynamic steering means making rapid, workable decisions, which are then tested and adjusted based on real data

If, like Rakesh, you are used to the "predict-and-control" model, this may feel like a loss of control. How do you manage such a process? And how do you know if you will achieve your objectives? More than anything, planning and controlling give you the *illusion* of control. In a complex, turbulent environment, the predict-and-control model breaks down quickly. You are far better off making a workable decision with incomplete information, which you then try out and adjust based on the feedback you get.

In fact, dynamic steering probably gives you more control, not less.

Dynamic steering is sometimes confused with chaos—"We're just going to try something and go from there." Nothing could be further from the truth: this approach requires more, not less, discipline than predicting and controlling! To begin with, it requires radical transparency regarding progress and priorities. Lacking transparency, you miss vital information needed for making the necessary adjustments. In addition, dynamic steering requires you to work in short cycles, instead of trying to predict the future upfront.

There is nothing wrong with looking ahead, but reality has a habit of obsoleting your plans! An annual planning cycle offers very little flexibility for making adjustments along the way. Holacracy replaces it with a number of shorter, highly reliable cycles. For operational work, this cycle can be as short as a day (daily stand-up) or a week (tactical meeting). Roles and accountabilities are adjusted in a monthly cycle (governance meeting). Finally, a circle's strategy is adjusted in a cycle averaging three to six months.

Dynamic steering only works when you have high transparency about the circle's current reality, triggering continuous adjustments

We still live and work in a "predict-and-control" world for the most part. Consider budgets, planning cycles, and accounting systems, but also employment contracts, performance evaluation, job descriptions, and compensation systems: they are all based on the predict-and-control model. There are many exciting experiments happening to bring more transparency and flexibility to each of these areas. This may not be the place to go into them in detail, but it may be worth taking a closer look at your own organization. Can you see any opportunities for more dynamic steering? What cycles could you shorten? And how can you introduce more transparency, so you can make continuous adjustments? Whatever the case, Holacracy gives you an "operating system" that has dynamic steering built-in!

THE SOLUTION

Neil gets out of the taxi and looks up. In a few meetings he will be somewhere up there, looking out over the riverfront. After the management team meeting, he and Rakesh had immediately booked a ticket to Portland for an emergency meeting with Denis. When they step out of the elevator, a secretary meets them and shows them the way to the conference room. Denis is sitting at the head of the long, egg-shaped table; his co-directors sit on either side of him.

"Welcome, welcome. We can't wait to hear what you have to tell us."

Neil looks at Rakesh. "Shall I do the talking this time?"

Rakesh nods. "Go ahead."

Neil walks to the front of the room and fires up his presentation. In about half an hour, he takes them through a detailed analysis of the campaign status in Canada, the United States, and Mexico, along with projections based on the latest statistics. His finishing statement is followed by silence, broken only by the sound of Denis' pen scratching on paper.

Denis looks up. "And this means ..."

Neil takes a deep breath. "This means that it will be difficult to achieve the July first deadline."

There is some mumbling on the other side of the table.

Denis looks uncomfortable. "Gentlemen, that is not what we agreed. You made a commitment. We expected you to deliver on it. How are you going to solve this problem?"

It is as Neil had feared. Denis puts the ball right back in their court. He glances over at Rakesh and then takes a step forward.

"Yes, we agreed with your ambitious plan. But as we got to work on the campaign, we learned many new things. For example, we have taken on a new online agency, which has given us a much better sense of what we can do online. And the initial results are above expectation in a number of regions."

That gets Denis' attention. "Which regions?"

"Particularly Canada and the Northwest and Southwest. Less so in Mexico and the eastern half of the U.S."

Neil's confidence is starting to build. He pauses for a moment before he continues.

"Denis, we have just given you a detailed overview of where we stand. But what is it that's most important for you?"

"Why do you ask?"

Neil replies, "In the past few months, we have transformed our way of working. We are now able to respond much more rapidly to changes and opportunities. So, if we know what your priorities are, we can adjust accordingly."

Denis sits up in his chair.

"Well, okay, now that you ask, our first priority is to launch in Canada and the Northwest, because we already have our operation up and running there."

"All right. So, may I take it that you are not yet fully operational in the eastern United States?"

Denis sighs. "Well ... not entirely. But we are working on it day and night."

Neil leafs through his papers.

"That's good, actually, because when I look at our data, I can see that your priority regions are also the regions where we are right on schedule, and where we will be able to launch on July first. He exchanges a quick look with Rakesh, who nods.

"So, I propose that we start in those countries on July first, and that we start up the other regions step by step. If we work closely together, we can make sure that the campaign is ready for launch as soon as you have your operations in place in each region."

For the first time, Neil sees a slight smile on Denis's face. He takes a moment to consult with his colleagues. Then he looks back at Neil and says,

"It's a deal."

RELIEF

N eil is happy with the new understanding that they managed to develop with the Portland office. After the meeting, they stuck around and talked with Denis for a while longer. They agreed to have a weekly teleconference to keep each other up to date on their progress.

Neil and his team work hard through the entire month of June. They continue to learn from the new online agency, while the increasing integration of TV raises the campaign to a whole new level. Being in continuous connection with Portland has created even more focus.

For all their busyness, Neil's department has become much quieter. Some days, their concentration is almost palpable. Every day, at exactly nine a.m., everyone present gathers for their daily stand-up. The weekly tactical meetings are a habit that they have all come to rely on. And while John spent some time supporting Soraya at first, she has become a competent Facilitator that has the circle's tactical and governance meetings well in hand.

○

On July 1, at exactly five p.m., the campaign launches in Canada and the Northwest. A launch party has been organized at the office in Seattle. The weather is warm, someone put on some music, and people are having drinks in the garden. The website went live an hour earlier and nearly collapsed under the huge number of visitors after the first commercials were broadcast. Fortunately,

Tamara had the foresight to make sure that there was plenty of extra server capacity. Neil is outside talking to John when his phone rings. He can't hear who it is and goes inside.

"Oh, Denis, it's you."

"We have a problem."

Neil's heart skips a beat.

"A problem?"

Denis laughs. "Our Customer Service department can't handle all the phone calls that are coming in!"

Neil breathes a sigh of relief. "That is what you might call a serious problem."

Denis says, "Neil, congratulations, man. I must say, your team has delivered excellent work and I am looking forward to continue to work with you."

Neil thanks Denis for the compliment.

What a relief! He feels the fatigue from all those months of hard work drain away. He walks back into the garden. At the makeshift bar he runs into Rakesh, who has a beer in his hand. Rakesh raises his bottle and gives him a big smile, "Congratulations, Neil! Good work!"

"It's the team that did it, not me."

Rakesh replies, "Right, of course you would say that. But you can take the credit you deserve."

"Thanks, Rakesh, but it's really true. It doesn't feel like just my accomplishment."

Rakesh nods. "Well, it's fantastic either way. Here's to your team!"

The music is turned up and Rakesh moves a little closer to Neil.

"You know, to tell you the truth, I had my doubts about what you were doing for a while there. Especially when Suzanne left, I was really scratching my head."

"I can totally understand that."

"For the longest time it looked like the team was really falling apart."

Neil agrees. "Yes, that's what it felt like. And for me, it was the reason for adopting Holacracy."

Rakesh takes a sip of his beer. "I've been hearing about it a lot and I'm getting more and more curious what it's all about. Maybe you can come tell the management team about it some time?"

Neil grins. "Sure, good idea!"

7.4 LOOKING BACK

They did it! After four intense months with many ups and downs, Neil and his team can now raise their glasses and celebrate the campaign launch. Time to look back! It all started with the deal in Portland. It was a great opportunity to show what Neil and his marketing team were capable of. But it was also a challenge, which required the team's productivity to be turned up a few notches. Initially, Neil had hoped to be able to make that jump in productivity with more management and control, based on his own way of working and inspired by the Getting Things Done method.

Meeting John however, had helped him see that team productivity is more than the sum of each team member's personal productivity.

Neil was intrigued when John told him about "Getting Things Done for teams." Could that help him raise his team's game to a higher level? He decided to try it. After John's presentation, Neil signed the Holacracy Constitution in front of his entire team and the implementation began!

During the first phase of the implementation, they described the roles in the marketing circle, based on how they worked at the time. As the circle's brand new Lead Link, it was Neil's accountability to then assign these roles.

After that, they were ready for the next step: the governance meeting. The first governance meeting certainly took some getting used to. The rigid structure left little room for discussion and John proved to be a strict Facilitator. Still, even in that first governance meeting, some proposals were accepted that created more clarity about the circle's roles and expectations. The word "tension" came up again and again, and turned out to be the fuel for improving the circle's role structure.

Once the roles had been described and the governance meetings kicked off, phase two of the implementation began: connecting the roles with their day-to-day work. The team learned that roles have a lot of freedom to make decisions autonomously, but that they are not without responsibility, too. In the workshop "Getting Roles Done," John introduced five basic responsibilities that came with taking on a role. Even though these responsibilities were relatively common sense, making them explicit helped them see that they were not yet common practice.

The weekly review, especially, was new for a lot of them. It required discipline, but also provided a sense of peace and focus!

In addition, the weekly review turned out to be a great way of preparing for the weekly tactical meeting—the last major piece of the Holacracy puzzle. Here, what everyone was working on became visible, through clear metrics and a project board with each role's key projects. If someone got stuck or a tension popped up, this was identified early on and immediately clarified into next-actions and new projects.

The circle also enjoyed their daily rhythm of short stand-up meetings. Those ten to fifteen minutes they spent together each morning saved them a lot of time during the day, which in the past they had spent on many short one-on-one's and a flood of emails to get aligned. An additional benefit was that they didn't have to interrupt each other's work flow as much during the day, so they were better able to concentrate on things that they barely had time for before.

After nearly four months, the new way of working now felt pretty normal. Soraya had taken over the Facilitator role from John and after just a few meetings of practice, she was already almost as strict. Will was elected as the circle's Secretary and was often complimented on the clarity of the governance and tactical meeting output. But the biggest transformation of all was without a doubt Neil's. Where before he had clung desperately to his predict-and-control management style, as Lead Link he had let go more and more. In the space created by the circle's increased clarity and productivity, he and his team were able to largely absorb the blow dealt to them by Suzanne's sudden departure.

Thinking in terms of tensions also felt more and more natural. Their roles and accountabilities had changed quite a bit after only a few governance meetings. Some roles were clarified, while others were split up. A number of roles that had been forgotten in the initial workshop a few months earlier were added later. Evolving their governance using tensions as fuel increasingly led to solutions and ideas that they would never have been able to come up with in the past. Before, they had never had that much transparency about what everyone was working on and how they were progressing. It had been an intense four months, but they made it in the end. The team—no, the circle—was more productive than ever!

7.5 PRACTICE MAKES PERFECT

The learning curve of a team that is new to Holacracy consists of two distinct phases. In the first phase (implementation), the emphasis is on the circle's meetings. After all, these are the most visible elements of Holacracy, and learning the rules of the governance and tactical meeting demand a lot of attention at first. There is a lot of emphasis on the circle's roles, particularly during the governance meeting, but also in the tactical meeting. During the second phase (integration), the attention begins to shift to what happens *outside* of the meetings. Roles become increasingly important in the way the circle works and communicates, not only during meetings, but also in the day-to-day work. This means that people start to exercise more autonomy and even entrepreneurship in the way they energize their roles, and begin to feel comfortable using the authority that comes with their roles to make their own decisions. The weekly review and other basic responsibilities of filling a role have now become habits that can be relied on.

In the implementation phase of Holacracy, the meetings are central, while in the integration phase, attention shifts from the meetings to working and collaborating from roles

But does that mean we're done? Or are we just getting started? Similar to Getting Things Done, Holacracy is not so much a model or a theory, but an ongoing practice. Unfortunately, this means that you are never quite done, but it also means that there is infinite potential to continue developing and deepening the practice. There is a reason people say "practice makes perfect"!

GTD veterans often say that the weekly review is the key to success. If you keep up this one habit, chances are your productivity will shoot up. The same is true for Holacracy. If you don't maintain it, you can easily slide back into old habits and patterns. Outside support can be of great help in escaping the gravitational pull of those old patterns, but you can't continue relying on that kind of "boost." So how do you make sure that the circle will sustain its high performance? And what are the biggest pitfalls?

The key points for sustaining your practice of Holacracy are:
- Rhythm and discipline
- The Facilitator role
- Connecting roles with the day-to-day work
- Onboarding new people

Rhythm and discipline

The first point may well be the most important one. The power of a habit is that you do it automatically, without even thinking about it. That is why it is so important to establish a reliable meeting rhythm. Think of it as the "heartbeat" of the circle: daily stand-ups, your own weekly review, followed by the tactical meeting, and a monthly governance meeting (or more often at first, if needed). Some teams have a different rhythm and choose to have some of these meetings more or less frequently. Once you've been doing it for a while, you will figure out what works best for your circle.

Establish a reliable meeting rhythm for your circle, so that it becomes a habit that you will not even have to think about

This is where the biggest pitfall often occurs, however. In every implementation there comes a time (often after three to six months) where you start to get more comfortable. Holacracy's rules and processes are beginning to fade into the background, and the circle's work once again takes center stage. Of course, this is not only normal, but also desirable. However, this is also the time when you may feel tempted to start skipping the odd governance meeting ("There aren't really any tensions right now"), or to slow down the meeting rhythm ("Once every two months seems like enough for us").

This gradual process of erosion not only threatens the meeting rhythm, but also the strictness of the meeting structure and rules, and the language that comes with them. It often starts out innocently: you skip something once, you take a quick shortcut, you react during a round where that would usually be cut off.

Of course, rhythm and structure are not goals in and of themselves. Sometimes there is a very good reason to do something differently. But the structure and the rules are also there to break a number of bad habits—discussing everything with everyone, constantly interrupting each other, not making decisions, and so on. You can compare the discipline of a reliable meeting rhythm and a rigid meeting structure to a river bed that channels your energy and attention. If you stretch or shift it too much, you may soon find yourself in a stagnant swamp.

The Facilitator role

It is the role of the Facilitator to enforce the rules and maintain the structure during the circle's tactical and governance meetings. You can compare it to playing sports. If the referee doesn't care much about the rules, or sometimes he does and sometimes he doesn't, things will quickly get out of hand. Before you know it, you are spending half your time talking about the rules of the game and whether or not the ball was out of bounds. With a good referee however, you can put all your energy into playing the game. It is the same with a good Facilitator: you can trust that every tension has its time and place, and there is a trusted process for doing something with it. As long as the Facilitator enforces the rules, nothing can really go wrong. If he doesn't, you can request a new Facilitator election in the next governance meeting, using the integrative election process.

Remember though, that even the best Facilitator can't do it alone. Playing by the rules is something you do as a circle, with the occasional reminder by the Facilitator. If you can rely on that, you will have found the key to relaxed productivity—not just on a personal level, but with the whole team playing in a state of flow!

The role of the Facilitator is to enforce the rules of Holacracy, so the circle can get into a state of flow

Connecting roles with the day-to-day work

Roles are at the heart of Holacracy. By having regular governance meetings, you make sure that this heart keeps pumping and that the roles continue to evolve based on tensions. But that is really just the beginning. If you only look at the circle's roles during the governance meeting, then your roles are no more than a paper reality. The place where roles really come to life is in the day-to-day work.

You are not your roles. You could say that you "play" your roles. So, in a way it is all "role play," although it is play with a serious goal: achieving the purpose of your role, of the circle, and of the organization as a whole. By energizing your role, you bring the organization closer to fulfilling its purpose. Your accountabilities describe what is expected of you, which you then translate into the projects and actions that make up your day-to-day work.

Roles are sometimes seen as theoretical descriptions that are relatively separate from daily work. In Holacracy however, it is rather the opposite—roles literally describe what is expected of you. Your roles and accountabilities drive the choices you make about how you will (and will not) spend your time. Is something part of your role or not? If not, then it cannot be expected of you. It is absolutely fine to do it occasionally, but watch out that you do not "rescue" the circle by picking it up on a more ongoing basis! Why? Because then you deprive the circle of an opportunity to create more ongoing (as opposed to ad hoc) clarity about its roles and expectations. So, practice saying "Not my role" more often and save those tensions for the agenda of the next governance meeting.

Roles literally define what is expected of you; use them as a guideline in the choices you make

The weekly review and the tactical meeting are also great opportunities to connect your roles with the daily work. During your weekly review, you check in with your roles and accountabilities to see which new projects and actions you want to pick up. This is how you energize your role in a proactive and entrepreneurial way, instead of waiting for outside stimuli to get you going in a more reactive way. The same applies to the tactical meeting: you can practice the circle's "role awareness" by continuously bringing the discussion back to roles. The focus should not be on "who," but on "which role."By taking your roles seriously and energizing them with awareness, you quickly bring tensions and lack of clarity to the surface. This is the fuel that the circle uses to continuously evolve the way it works, so it can go back to playing the game from ever-more clarity and flow!

Onboarding new people

The last thing to keep in mind to maintain your Holacracy practice is how you deal with new people. Holacracy is a very different way of working, with new habits and new language, such as "tensions" and "workable" decisions. When new people join the team, you will be reminded of how different it really is. At first, they will likely be quite surprised at the way meetings are run. It is important, therefore, to onboard them well; in other words, help them get adjusted to Holacracy's way of working. You can't expect them to learn to play a new game without spending at least some time explaining the rules! If you try anyway, you run the risk of gradually sliding back with each new team member, until you find yourself back where you started. The Facilitator can often play an important role in the onboarding process, because this role is so familiar with the structure of the meetings and the principles of Holacracy.

EIGHT

HOLACRACY FOR THE ORGANIZATION

8.1 SCALING UP TO MULTIPLE CIRCLES

In this book, we have presented Holacracy as a method for team productivity. But a productive team does not automatically translate into a productive organization (unless the organization consists of just one team). A team is part of a larger whole. The challenges that come with collaboration and alignment *within* the team also apply *between* teams. In many cases, they are even more complex.In a conventional organization, tackling this is the task of management. Authority is centralized in the role of the manager, who plans and manages.

As we have just seen, Holacracy uses a very different approach. Authority is distributed to the circle's roles, which operate autonomously in order to achieve the desired outcomes. The alignment between these roles is not done by a centralized role (such as a manager), but is built into the circle's meetings.

To give a few examples of this distributed authority: roles report to the circle, they set their own priorities, and they make these transparent to the rest of the circle (using the project board). Everyone has the power to propose changes to how authority is distributed (during the governance meeting), the agenda for a meeting is built together, and roles are accountable to each other for their work. The Lead Link does have a number of significant accountabilities, but it is far from the centralized role of the conventional manager.

A team running with Holacracy within a larger, convention-al organization will therefore inevitably run into challenges, as il-lustrated by

the friction in the relationship between Neil and Rakesh. If you wanted to use these tensions as fuel for continuous improve-ment, you would need to scale up Holacracy beyond one team. But how do you go about that? How do you spread Holacracy to multiple teams, or even to the organization as a whole?

This touches on a part of Holacracy that we have not yet dealt with in this book—how do circles work together to achieve the goals of the organization? Holacracy is not just for teams; it's even more powerful at the organizational level! Although we cannot fully do justice to this subject here, we would like to at least paint you a high-level overview of Holacracy for the organization.

Organic circle structure

Until now we have focused on what happens within the circle. But suppose there are multiple circles, each of which works according to the rules of Holacracy. How do they work together? And how do you make sure that expectations between circles become as clear as between the roles within each circle?

An organization running Holacracy has a nested structure of circles and sub-circles that are connected by means of double links.

To really understand Holacracy's circle structure, we need to go back to the meaning of the term Holacracy: governance (*-cracy*) by the *holarchy*.

A holarchy refers to a natural hierarchy, such as the body, which consists of organs, which in turn consist of cells, or a sen-tence, which consists of words, which in turn consist of letters.

With Holacracy, the organizational structure consists of a holarchy of circles and sub-circles, which are connected through double links

With Holacracy, the organization consists of circles, which in turn are made up of sub-circles. Just like an organ in a body, the circle performs a certain function for the organization. A circle operates with high autonomy, but at the same time it is also part of a greater whole. Each circle covers a particular area of work of the organization. An area of work may refer to, for example, a product or a department. The work of a circle can be broken down into smaller areas of work, which in turn are controlled and managed by autonomous sub-circles.

An example will help to make this clear. The marketing circle controls the work of marketing all the organization's products. Each product constitutes an area of work, which is managed by a sub-circle of the marketing circle. Each sub-circle is accountable for marketing that specific product. The marketing circle itself is in turn part of a broader circle: the company circle. In this way, the organization operates as an organic structure of circles and sub-circles,each with a well-defined scope of work to control and manage.

Each circle controls and manages an area of work, and may in turn be broken down into sub-circles which are accountable for smaller areas of work

A traditional organization chart can often serve as a good starting point for the circle structure of an organization. It is only a starting point though, because each circle has full autonomy and authority to organize and manage itself. This means that a circle may decide to create a new sub-circle without having to involve the "higher" circle in the decision. The circle structure is therefore not designed from the top down, but evolves through an organic, distributed process. As we've seen, this occurs during each circle's regular governance meetings, which define and evolve not only the circle's roles, but also its sub-circles.

A situation involving multiple circles is therefore not fundamentally different from one with a single circle, which has been the focus of this book. In both situations, the governance meeting is the key process which distributes accountability and authority, not only into roles, but also into circles and sub-circles.

Connecting circles

Circles are organized in a natural hierarchy (holarchy) of expanding scope, from circles with a broad domain, to sub-circles with a narrower sub-domain. But that does not address the question of how these circles are connected. In conventional organizations, this connection is established by the manager or supervisor, who connects two organizational levels.

Holacracy uses a variation on this solution: each circle is connected to both its "higher" circle and its sub-circles by means of double links. This double link is established by defining two core roles: the Lead Link and the Rep Link.

These roles ensure a two-way flow of information and tensions at all levels of the organization. The Lead Link is appointed by the higher circle and represents the circle and its needs in the sub-circle. The other half of the double link is formed by the role of Rep Link (an abbreviation of "representative"). The Rep Link represents the sub-circle and its needs in the higher circle. Both the Lead Link and the Rep Link participate in the meetings of both circles. The Lead Link concentrates on the alignment of the circle's work with the goals and needs of the higher circle. The Rep Link brings the perspective of the sub-circle to the meetings of the higher circle, so that information and tensions can be integrated into the decision-making at that level.

Circles are connected by means of a double link, formed by the roles of Lead Link and Rep Link, which ensure a two-way flow of communication and alignment

This double link exists on all levels of the organization and guarantees a smooth flow of information in both directions. It also ensures that tensions that are identified in one part of the organization can be channeled to the relevant circle quickly and effectively. In this way, it is possible to use Holacracy not only within one or multiple teams, but as a comprehensive management system for the organization as a whole.

8.2 THE NEXT STEP

You are a unique sensor for the roles, the team, and the organization you work in. Your attention is automatically drawn to gaps between how things are now and how they could be, possibly even while you read this book! Maybe it has helped you to see your current situation with new eyes. And hopefully it has provided you with inspiration about what is possible in your team or organization. Whether the things drawing your attention are big or small, they are each a tension. And the big question is: what are you going to do with those tensions when you've finished reading this book?

Tensions contain energy that can be used to put something into motion. Holacracy's promise is that you can set up the team or even the entire organization in such a way that you can use *every* tension as fuel for continuous improvement. But how do you make that promise come to life? How do you use the tensions you sense to take a step forward? To start with, let's see if we can clarify these tensions. Do you remember the clarifying questions you can ask yourself to figure out what to do with a tension?

- Does your role care?
- Does another role within your circle care?
- Does your circle care?
- Does the organization care?
- Do you care personally?

Now it gets interesting! Some readers will conclude that the tensions they sense about the current way of working and the possibilities offered by Holacracy do indeed belong to their roles. Others will find that it is "not their role," but that there is another role or circle within the organization that they could talk to about it. Finally, there may be some of you who do not have a clear place for the tensions you sense in your team or organization. In those cases, the last question remains: do you care personally? If you have read this far, the answer to that question is likely "yes"! So do you want to start using your tensions as fuel for change, either personally or within your organization? Fantastic!

Be the change

Do you think that your team or organization is not ready for distributed authority? Or that there is no room to even experiment with this kind of approach? Then be the change you wish to see! To be clear: adopting Holacracy all by yourself is impossible. After all, it is a method for *team* productivity. What you *can* do is use elements of the method to lead by example and to create more clarity for yourself. Here are some examples of what you can do with the material provided in this book:

- Maintain a complete overview of all your current next-actions and projects. Empty your mind and give everything a place in this external memory. Start a "waiting for" list with outstanding and delegated tasks for you follow up on. Make it a habit to formulate clear next-actions and desired outcomes and offer to keep an action list during team meetings. Read David Allen's book *Getting Things Done* to gain more insight into how you can build an effective system that will provide you with a dynamic and crystal-clear overview of your own work (see Appendix 1 for a short summary).

- Suggest a different way to do your regular operational meeting, with you as the facilitator. Start with a check-in, followed by a round of brief updates about what everyone is working on. Then build the agenda together and emphasize that everyone is welcome to contribute items. Make sure that all the agenda items are dealt with within the allotted time. You do this by continually focusing on what the owner of the item needs and what the next-action is . Ask someone to write these down on an action list, including the name of the person that is going to take the next-action. Spend the last five minutes of the meeting on the check-out, so that everyone can share their reflection of how it went!

- Propose maintaining a physical project board to create more transparency about what everyone is working on and how they are progressing. Introduce the definition of a project as a desired outcome, formulated as if it had already been accomplished (for example, "Project board created and populated"). Review it together every day, or at least every week (maybe in a stand-up or tactical meeting), and do a round of updates.

- Suggest a different way of dealing with complex subjects, then introduce the integrative decision-making process. Ask someone to prepare a proposal (one or two paragraphs, not a multi-page document). Ask permission to cut people off if necessary. Start with a round of clarifying questions. Then ask everyone in turn for a short reaction to the proposal. Finally, do an objection round: is the proposal workable, or do you see a specific reason why we can't try it, at least for a while? Write down any objections and use them to make the proposal workable during the integration round; follow this up with a new objection round. If there are no (further) objections, the proposal has been accepted!

- Keep track of your daily activities for a few weeks and use that to describe your roles and accountabilities. Compare this to your job description (if there is one) and go over it with your manager and your team. Ask them for feedback, or better yet, ask them what they expect from you (preferably in clear accountabilities, starting with a verb, such as "Maintaining the website"). Offer to do the same for them, individually or in a joint session about mutual expectations (see Chapter 3 for this).

Implementing Holacracy

Would you like to go a step further and adopt Holacracy in your team? Is your manager prepared to experiment with distributed authority? And does the team actually have a shared purpose that they need to work together to achieve? Then you can turn your team into a circle!

The ideal size of a circle is six to eight people, although it generally works well enough with anything from four to ten people. If there are fewer people, you might ask yourself if it is truly necessary to introduce much fomal structure. If there are more than eight to ten, you will find that the meetings will take longer and will be more challenging. In addition, sub-groups will often emerge naturally, signalling that you may actually be dealing with more than one circle.

Let's go over the implementation steps again for a minute. The first step is the formal adoption of the Holacracy Constitution by the current powerholder(s), often the manager. By signing this, the manager signals a willingness and intent to let go of his or her authority to control and manage the team. This authority is now transferred to the circle's governance meeting, where it will be determined how accountabilities and authorities will be distributed from then on. The former powerholder usually takes on the role of Lead Link in the circle.

This is a big step, but at the same time, it is just the beginning.

The next step is to define the initial structure of roles and accountabilities. Since these will be continuously adjusted during governance meetings, it is enough to establish a workable starting point. The quickest and easiest way to identify the initial roles is by making the current reality explicit. What is already being done and what actions and accountabilities belong together naturally? You can find step-by-step instructions for doing this in Chapter 3.

Publish the initial structure in a medium (physical or digital) that everyone has easy access to. Because roles and accountabilities change after each governance meeting, it is important to keep this overview up-to-date. A shared document may be sufficient, but you can also use software that guides you through Holacracy's meetings and automatically saves the meeting outcomes (see Appendix 2).

Time for the first governance meeting! The Lead Link assigns a temporary Facilitator until the circle elects a regular Facilitator and Secretary later in the same meeting. Together, build an agenda based on tensions and process each tension using the steps of the integrative decision-making process. End with a check-out to give everyone the opportunity to share his or her reflections of the first governance meeting! Ask the newly elected Secretary to schedule a regular rhythm of weekly tactical meetings and bi-weekly governance meetings (later, monthly may be more appropriate).

Next, create a project board in preparation of the first tactical meeting, either physical or digital, with all the circle members' current projects on it.

The elected Facilitator leads the tactical meeting and the Secretary records the next-actions and projects. In the beginning, pay extra attention to metrics and project rounds. Once those run smoothly, you will find that tensions are sensed more early on and can be acted upon immediately!

Done? Then the circle is now operating holacratically! The real jump in clarity and productivity will come with continuing practice, so make sure you maintain your meeting rhythm. In the previous chapters, we have mentioned a number of tips and pitfalls that may be worth reviewing after a few weeks or months. If you remember only one thing, remember the principle of "tough love", which applies to everyone but most of all to the circle's Facilitator. Holacracy meetings have a high degree of discipline and structure, which are actively enforced by the Facilitator. If you have a Facilitator who is casual about this, or who finds it difficult to cut people off when necessary, the meetings will gradually lose their built-in power and clarity!

The promise of Getting Teams Done

The basic premise of this book is that team productivity is more than the sum of individual productivity. However, the reverse is also true: team productivity is no guarantee for individual productivity. The promise of Getting Teams Done, therefore, is the combination of individual and team productivity. David Allen, the creator and writer of *Getting Things Done*, decided to adopt Holacracy in his own company in 2011. He calls the combination of GTD and Holacracy a "one-two punch": together they allow for a quantum leap in productivity!

Just like GTD creates a trusted system for your individual work, Holacracy creates one for the work of the team and the organization as a whole. You know exactly what is expected of you and what you are accountable for. You can use all your energy and creativity to drive your roles forward, instead of wasting endless time and energy on politics and drama. There is no need to try to build consensus all the time, because within your own roles you have the autonomy to make decisions. You lead your roles, knowing that others are leading theirs.

Meanwhile, the organization's sensors are becoming increasingly sensitive to tensions and things that are not going as they should or could.

As more clarity is created, more space opens up for noticing things that are working ok, but that could be even better. The circle is constantly engaged in multiple, smaller and bigger experiments by making workable decisions and field-testing them in a disciplined way.

New ideas come out of the most unexpected corners and instantly flow to the relevant role, instead of falling prey to politics or endless meetings. The language of tensions, workable decisions, and "no objection" increasingly permeates the culture of the organization and replaces the language of problems, blame, and mistakes. You make the best of everyone's skills and talents, and, because of the clear distinction between roles and persons, everyone can be fully themselves.

And just when you think you have reached the top of the mountain, you will find that you are just getting started. The higher you climb, the more you see. There is one thing you will never have to worry about—no matter how far you travel, you will always have access to an infinite source of energy: tension. We wish you much fuel!

THE SEQUEL?

When Neil walks into the boardroom, the entire management team is already seated. He sits down and Rakesh opens the meeting.

"Neil, once again, kudos from all of us—excellent work! We would like you to tell us more about Holacracy. Could you give us a brief explanation of what it is and how you and your team used it?"

Neil looks up. "What it is ... hmm ... It's not easy to explain in a few words. It is a method, a way of thinking ... Well, anyway, it is something that you have to practice for a while before you can really understand it."

Rakesh says, impatiently, "What I really want to know ... You guys managed to come up with a surprisingly good result in a short time. I think there are more teams in this organization that could benefit from this approach."

Neil smiles. "I think so too."

Rakesh continues, "What I'd like to ask you is, do you think you could help other teams adopt Holacracy?"

Neil thinks for a moment.

"Well?"

Neil says, "I have thought about this before ... So yes, I think so."

"Great."

"But you could even take it a step further."

Rakesh asks, "What do you mean?"

"If you really want to experience the power of Holacracy, I think the best thing would be to implement it in the entire organization."

"Yes, that is what I meant. Are you, or is your team, willing to coach all the other teams?"

"Well, what I meant is the *entire* organization, so including upper management."

All is quiet for a moment.

Rakesh frowns. "That is something else. You mean we should also adopt this way of working?"

"Exactly."

"Why do you think so?"

Neil explains that Holacracy is a type of management system that can be applied to teams, but which will lead to even greater clarity and productivity at the organizational level. He goes on to say,

"And then we would be able to break through to a whole new level."

Rakesh asks him, "Suppose I wanted to do this as soon as possible. Could I just make that decision, as the CEO?"

Neil laughs. "That would be your last act as a heroic leader."

"Excuse me?"

Neil explains, "Just kidding. Yes, you could."

"And you could do this in five months?"

Neil immediately senses a tension. He thinks about the presentation in Portland where it all began ... *here we go again.* "Shall we talk to John first, before we give ourselves a new deadline?"

Rakesh answers, "Sure. Can you invite him as soon as possible?"

Smiling, Neil says, "No objection; that seems workable to me."

ABOUT THE AUTHORS

DIEDERICK JANSE is a certified Holacracy master coach and co-founding partner at Energized.org, which helps organizations make the leap to radical self-management. As co-founder of the Waking Up the Workplace interview series, he developed an online training course about the future of work, which included David Allen, author of *Getting Things Done* (*GTD*).

Diederick earned a degree in International Business in 2006 and has worked with IBM, Springest, Shell, Voys, Rockstart, Greenpeace, and the worldwide Impact Hub network. He is a veteran GTD practitioner and has worked together with Holacracy pioneer Brian Robertson for over ten years. Diederick lives in Utrecht, The Netherlands with his wife and two daughters.

MARCO BOGERS is certified Holacracy®, True Purpose® and Productivity Coach, supporting individuals and organizations on their Self Management journey. He has worked with organizations in diverse sectors, ranging from corporates and governments to innovative tech startups. His mission is to ignite a healing fire in leaders and organizations who are called to make a difference in the world. Prior to becoming a coach he had senior positions within international tech companies like Canon and France Telecom. He lives with his family in the Netherlands.

GETTING THINGS DONE

Getting Things Done (GTD) is a personal productivity method for managing agreements, information, and communication. It was created by U.S. author David Allen, who wrote the 2001 book by the same name. The method has been embraced by millions worldwide and has become the norm at many organizations.

The essence of Getting Things Done is that you maintain an external system outside of your head. The system is set up in such a way that you can trust that you are making the right choices in the moment. This keeps your mind free, so that you can work from a place of peace and relaxation.

David Allen is often compared to Stephen Covey, the author of *The 7 Habits of Highly Effective People*, the most successful management book ever. But where Covey's approach begins by defining a personal mission statement, which is then translated into a weekly and daily plan, Allen's starting point is to gain control of even the smallest details. This means that for most people, GTD starts with something "boring," like cleaning up your desk, file cabinet, or mailbox. But that is just the beginning.

Despite the sobering practicality of Allen's approach, the method has a number of surprisingly profound effects when put into practice. Experienced GTD practitioners:

- **Experience less stress** because they have learned to empty their minds.
- **Are more creative** because their minds are not crowded with trivial issues.

- **Are better able to concentrate** because they always consciously choose what to work on. This allows them to resist their own impulses and interruptions from others.
- **Experience more "flow,"** because they are constantly training to make quick, intuitive decisions.
- **Work faster**, because they have organized their own workflow in such a way that friction has been reduced to a minimum.

To be effective in your work and your life, Allen believes, you need two things: *control* and *perspective*. Compare this to driving a car: you keep your hands on the steering wheel and your eyes on the road.

Control is about getting a grip on those things that you have not yet made a conscious decision about, but which you feel that you have to do something about (David Allen calls this *stuff*; in this book we call them *tensions*).

Achieving control is a continuous process that consists of five steps:

1. Capturing: You gather all your "stuff" (emails, thoughts, paper) together systematically in a trusted place (your inbox).
2. Clarifying: Next, you make a decision about what you want to do with each individual item.
3. Organizing: You save the outcome of those decisions in an external system, outside of your head.
4. Reviewing: You make sure that your system stays up-to-date, and you take a step back for reflection at regular intervals.
5. Doing: You make quick, intuitive decisions in the moment about what you are going to do, based on your context,

available time, energy level, and priority.

Perspective is where you are going. It is about gaining more and more clarity on all levels of your work and life. Gaining clarity means that you continually increase your sense of what is most important to you (priority). Allen talks about the type of conversation that you regularly need to have with yourself for each of these levels:

1. What should I do now? (Next-actions)
2. What do I need to complete? (Projects)
3. What do I need to maintain? (Roles and accountabilities, or areas of focus)
4. What do I want to accomplish? (Goals and objectives)
5. What does my ideal work and life look like? (Vision)
6. Why am I here? (Purpose and principles)

HOLACRACY

This appendix contains a number of useful overviews that you can use when implementing Holacracy. You will also find a detailed description of the accountabilities of the four core roles: Lead Link, Rep Link, Facilitator, and Secretary.

Holacracy* was developed by Brian Robertson and is a registered trademark of HolacracyOne, a U.S.-based organization that offers Holacracy training and implementation services.

For more information about Holacracy, the Holacracy Constitution, software, and support in implementing Holacracy, please visit holacracy.org.

Governance meeting

The structure of the governance meeting:

- Check-in – A short round in which everyone takes a turn sharing what is on their mind, so that they can let it go and be fully present. No discussion.
- Building the agenda – Build an agenda based on tensions, on the spot. One or two keywords per agenda items. No discussion.
- Item 1 – Process each agenda item using the steps of the integrative decision-making process (see below).
- Item 2
- Etc.
- Check-out – A short round in which everyone takes a turn

sharing their reflections and learnings, to mark the end of the meeting. No discussion.

Integrative decision-making

The integrative decision-making steps that are used to process agenda items in the governance meeting:

- Proposal – The owner of the agenda item explains the tension and makes a proposal. No questions or reactions.
- Clarifying questions – Anyone can ask the proposer questions to better understand the proposal. Only the proposer can respond, and "I don't know" or "Not specified in my proposal" are perfectly valid answers. No discussion.
- Reaction round – A round where everyone, except the proposer, gives a short reaction to the proposal. No discussion.
- Amend or clarify – The proposer can optionally amend or clarify the proposal. No discussion.
- Objection round – The Facilitator asks everyone, including the proposer, to answer with "Objection" or "No objection" to the proposal. Objections are captured and, if necessary, tested for their validity by the Facilitator. No discussion. If there are no objections, the proposal is accepted.
- Integration – The purpose of the integration step is to integrate each of the objections into a workable proposal. The initiative lies with the proposer and the objector(s); others may help. As soon as the Facilitator has checked whether the amended proposal addresses the objections and still solves the proposer's original tension, a new objection round follows.

Testing objections

Objections can be tested by the Facilitator using the following criteria to determine whether they are valid:

1. The proposal causes harm (it is not workable).
2. The objection follows directly from the proposal (it is created by it).
3. The objection is based on data (as opposed to a fear or prediction of what might happen - except when you know you will not be able to revisit the proposal before significant harm could occur, because then predicting the future is the smart thing to do).
4. The proposal limits one of the objector's roles
5. An objection that the proposal breaks the rules of Holacracy (as defined in the Holacracy Constitution) is always deemed valid. An example of this is a proposal to make a decision that falls outside of the circle's authority.

Weekly review

The weekly review is a "meeting with yourself" to empty your mind and to keep your action and project lists complete and current. You can use the following structure:

- Collecting – List
- all your tensions and open loops, e.g. by using the following 'trigger list':
  —Notes, voicemails, papers, downloads, etc.
  —Your unprocessed email of the last 1-2 weeks
  —Your agenda for the past 1-2 weeks
  —Your agenda for the coming 2-3 weeks
  —Your "waiting for" list
  —Your "someday/maybe" list

—Your current roles and accountabilities (at least once a month)

—Your mind (everything that has your attention and that you have to or want to do something about)

- Clarifying and organizing – For each item on your list, ask yourself the following questions:

  —Do any of your roles care? If so, clarify the next-action, and if applicable, the desired outcome (project). If not, pass it on to the right role or circle, put it on your "someday/maybe" list, or let it go.

  —If it takes less than two minutes to solve a tension, do it immediately (because in that case, clarifying and organizing would likely take more time than simply doing it right away).

- Maintaining –

- Now run through your various lists to make sure they are complete and current:

  —Actions (Are they clear?)

  —Projects (Is the desired outcome clear? Is it still correct? Is there at least one next-action for every project on your action list?)

  —Roles and accountabilities (Do they still reflect reality? Do you want to pick up any new projects? Do you have any agenda items for the governance meeting?)

  —Waiting for (Are they still current? Is there something you need to follow up on?)

  —Someday/maybe (Is there something you want to activate? Is there anything you can take off this list?)

- Prioritizing – Finish your weekly review by asking yourself these questions:

—How are you going to divide your energy and attention among your roles, projects, and actions? What are you going to do now and what can you do later? Use guidelines such as circle strategies and priorities in your choices, if appropriate.

—Run through your project list and select the projects you want to work on this week. Don't forget to update the circle's project board!

Tactical meeting

The structure of the tactical meeting:

- Check-in – A short round in which everyone takes a turn sharing what is on their minds, so that they can let it go and be fully present. No discussion.

- Checklist review – The Facilitator runs through the list of recurring tasks; the relevant roles indicate with a simple "Yes" or "No" whether or not the task has been carried out during the preceding time period. No discussion.

- Metrics review – Roles each take a turn reporting on the metrics assigned to them for the preceding time period. No discussion, though clarifying questions are allowed. Project updates – Circle members each give a short update about the progress of current projects in the preceding time period. No discussion.

- Agenda-building – Create an agenda on the spot, based on tensions. One or two keywords per agenda item, with one clear owner. No discussion.

—Item 1 – Process all the agenda items within the available time, one tension at a time, from one person at a time. The owner describes the tension and what he or she needs.

Others may help by asking questions or providing input. Each agenda item is completed by determining the next-action or project, if applicable.

—Item 2

—Etc.

- Check-out – A short round in which everyone takes a turn sharing their reflections and learnings, to mark the end of the meeting. No discussion.

Implementation steps

Below are the (simplified) steps of a Holacracy implementation within a team. For more details, see the relevant chapters in this book.

- Formally accept the Holacracy Constitution (you can find it at holacracy.org)
- Map out the initial roles and accountabilities based on the team's current reality
- Publish the initial roles and accountabilities in some system that the whole team can access
- Run the first governance meeting and elect a Facilitator and Secretary
- Create a project board with the current projects per role on it
- Run the first tactical meeting and define checklist items and metrics
- Ask the Secretary to schedule a regular rhythm of governance and tactical meetings

Core roles in Holacracy

The simplified description of the core roles below is based on version 4.1 of the Holacracy Constitution. Go to holacracy.org for the complete and most recent version of the Constitution.

LEAD LINK, accountable for:
- Distributing and organizing the circle's work into clear roles and policies
- Assigning roles to circle members, monitoring role fit, and reassigning roles to increase rol fit
- Allocating the circle's resources across its projects and roles
- Defining strategies and priorities for the circle
- Defining and assigning metrics that provide insight into the performance of the circle

REP LINK, accountable for:
- Providing visibility into the circle's health to the super-circle
- Processing tensions from the circle in the super-circle

FACILITATOR, accountable for:
- Facilitating the circle's governance and tactical meetings according to the rules of Holacracy (as defined in the Holacracy Constitution)

SECRETARY, accountable for:
- Scheduling the circle's governance and tactical meetings
- Capturing valid outcomes of the circle's governance and tactical meetings
- Maintaining a complete and current overview of the circle's roles and policies

GLOSSARY

Below you can find explanations for some of the most commonly used terms in this book.

ACCOUNTABILITY: An ongoing activity that can be expected from a role, giving the person filling the role full authority to take any action and make any decision he or she deems necessary to fulfill the accountability.

AUTHORITY: The right to take an action or make a decision on behalf of the organization.

BASIC RESPONSIBILITY: A general responsibility that comes with filling any role, apart from the specific accountabilities that have been defined for each individual role.

CHECK-IN: A short round in which everyone takes a turn sharing what is on their minds, so that they can let it go and be fully present. No discussion.

CHECK-OUT: A short round in which everyone takes a turn sharing their reflections and learnings, to mark the end of the meeting. No discussion.

CIRCLE STRUCTURE: An organic structure of circles and sub-circles, which are connected by means of double links (see below).

CIRCLE: A part of the organization that consists of roles and that fulfills a specific purpose within the organization.

CLARIFYING QUESTION: A question aimed at better understanding the proposal, during the clarifying questions step of the integrative decision-making process in the governance meeting.

CONSTITUTION: A document containing the core rules and processes of Holacracy, including the rights, duties, and authority of the roles and people involved. It is formally ratified by means of a signature of the duly authorized powerholder, providing the foundation for a Holacracy implementation. The complete version can be found at holacracy.org.

DESIRED OUTCOME: A desired result that requires more than one action to achieve.

DISTRIBUTED AUTHORITY: A situation where accountabilities and authority are broken down into circles and roles, that operate autonomously to fulfill their purpose.

DISTRIBUTED LEADERSHIP: A situation where leadership is expressed from within well-defined roles with specific accountabilities and authority. This means that everyone leads and follows at different times, depending on the topic. Distributed leadership is the opposite of centralized leadership, where management and leadership are concentrated in one or a few roles, such as, for example, the CEO, manager, or team lead.

DOMAIN: An organizational asset or activity controlled exclusively by a circle or role.

DOUBLE LINK: The connection between a circle and a sub-circle, consisting of two roles: the Lead Link, appointed by the (Lead Link of) the circle, and the Rep Link, elected by the sub-circle.

DYNAMIC STEERING: A process of continuous adaptation and improvement, fueled by tensions (in contrast to predict-and-control, which is based on assumptions and predictions).

FACILITATOR: Core role, assigned via the integrative elections process, which facilitates the governance and tactical meetings of the circle.

GETTING THINGS DONE: A method for individual productivity, from a place of relaxation and with an empty mind.

GOVERNANCE MEETING: A regular meeting in which the circle makes workable decisions about its roles and accountabilities, policies, and elections of the elected roles. It has a fixed format in which the agenda is created on the spot on the basis of tensions, and each agenda item is processed using integrative decision-making.

HEROIC LEADERSHIP: A pattern of taking personal responsibility, outside of formal roles and accountabilities. It deprives the organization of the need and the opportunity to formulate a structural solution for a particular tension or challenge.

HOLACRACY: A framework for team and organizational productivity, based on distributed authority and using tensions as fuel for continuous improvement.

IMPLEMENTATION: the process of adopting Holacracy, starting with the ratification of the Constitution, continuing with mapping the initial circles, roles, and accountabilities ,and learning the rules and processes of Holacracying, including fully distributed authority and regular governance and tactical meetings.

INDIVIDUAL ACTION: A conscious choice to take action outside of existing roles. If it becomes a pattern, it must be brought to the circle's governance meeting so it can be processed into a more structural solution (e.g. a role).

INTEGRATION: A step in the integrative decision-making process, which is used in the governance meeting to process tensions. The purpose of this step is to integrate valid objections into a proposal that is safe enough to try, which is determined in a follow-up objection round.

INTEGRATIVE DECISION-MAKING: A decision-making process that consists of a number of steps and that is used in the governance meeting to process tensions. Its purpose is to integrate relevant perspectives into workable decisions about roles and accountabilities, policies, and elections for the elected roles of the circle.

INTEGRATIVE ELECTIONS: A decision-making process that consists of a number of steps and is used in the governance meeting to elect the person that is the best fit for each of the circle's elected roles (Rep Link, Facilitator, and Secretary).

LEAD LINK: A core role that is appointed by the Lead Link of the higher circle, and is accountable for the circle fulfilling its purpose. Together with the Rep Link, the Lead Link constitutes the double link with the higher circle. The Lead Link has a number of specific accountabilities, which include assigning roles and allocating the circle's resources.

METRIC: A quantitative or qualitative indicator that provides insight into the health and performance of the circle. Metrics are reported during the tactical meeting.

NEXT-ACTION: The next physical action to decrease a tension or achieve a desired outcome.

NOMINATION: A recommendation for the person deemed the best fit for one of the circle's elected roles.

OBJECTION: A reasonable argument why a proposal causes harm or moves the circle backward.

PREDICT-AND-CONTROL: A way of thinking and a process in which a detailed plan is created upfront, based on assumptions and predictions about the future, which is then followed by a controlled execution of the planned steps (the opposite of "Dynamic steering").

PRIORITY: A conscious choice or explicit guideline about what is most important in light of the purpose of a specific role, circle, or the organization as a whole.

PROJECT BOARD: A visual overview of the circle's most relevant, ongoing projects. The project board creates transparency about the progress and priorities of the circle's work.

PROJECT: A desired outcome that requires more than one action to achieve.

PROJECTION: A realistic estimate about when you expect to finish something, based on a complete and current overview of all your commitments (in contrast to a blind promise).

PROPOSAL: A suggestion to change the way the circle operates, which if accepted, will solve or reduce a specific tension. It is the first step in the integrative decision-making process, which is used to process agenda items during the governance meeting. The person who adds the tension to the agenda is the proposer.

REACTION: A brief response to the proposal during the reaction round of the integrative decision-making process at the governance meeting.

REP LINK: A core role that is assigned by means of the integrative election process. The Rep Link represents the circle in meetings of the higher circle. Together with the Lead Link, the Rep Link constitutes the double link with the higher circle.

ROLE LEADERSHIP: Working and leading from within explicit, well-defined roles, using the authority of the role to take action and make decisions autonomously in order to fulfill the role's purpose and accountabilities (in contrast to "Heroic leadership").

ROLE: A part of the organization that fulfills a specific purpose within the organization and has specific accountabilities. A role is part of a circle, is defined in the circle's governance meeting, and is assigned to a member of the circle by the Lead Link.

SECRETARY: A core role that is assigned by means of the integrative election process. The Secreary schedules the governance and tactical meetings of the circle, records the meeting output, and maintains a current overview of the roles and policies of the circle.

SENSOR: A detection device which, in the context of Holacracy, refers to people's capacity to sense tensions, each with their own unique background and perspective.

STAND-UP: A short, daily meeting in which circle members share progress and identify tensions, all while standing up.

TACTICAL MEETING: A regular meeting in which the circle syncs up about its progress and priorities. It has a fixed format, in which the agenda is created on the spot on the basis of tensions, each of which is rapidly clarified and processed into next-actions and projects, if applicable.

TEAM: A group of people working together to achieve a common goal (unlike a circle, which consists of roles rather than people).

TENSION: The experience of a gap between how things are now and how they could be. Tension contains information and energy that can be used as fuel to move the organization closer to its purpose.

VALID OBJECTION: An objection that meets the criteria as defined in the Holacracy Constitution.

WAITING-FOR LIST: A list of all outstanding requests and items for which you are waiting for something or someone. It is part of a "trusted system", as described in Getting Things Done.

WEEKLY REVIEW: Weekly "meeting with yourself" to empty your mind and update your trusted system of projects and actions. It is particularly helpful in making proactive choices about what you will and will not be doing, instead of continuously reacting to the latest and loudest.

WORKABLE: Good enough and safe enough to try, knowing there is (almost) always an opportunity to make adjustments later, if necessary. This concept helps lower the threshold for decision-making and encourages experimentation and rapid iteration (in contrast to 'perfect forever' decisions that are based on assumptions and predictions about the future).

CPSIA information can be obtained
at www.ICGtesting.com
Printed in the USA
BVHW081504201021
619445BV00004B/29